A MANUAL FOR CHURCH LEADERS

CHRISTIAN VIEW OF SEX EDUCATION

By

MARTIN F. WESSLER

EDITOR / W. J. FIELDS

Concordia Publishing House
Saint Louis London

BOOK SIX of the Concordia Sex Education Series

Other titles in the series:

BOOK ONE: I WONDER, I WONDER

BOOK TWO: WONDERFULLY MADE

BOOK THREE: TAKE THE HIGH ROAD

BOOK FOUR: LIFE CAN BE SEXUAL

BOOK FIVE: PARENTS GUIDE TO CHRISTIAN CONVERSATION ABOUT SEX

Third Printing 1968

Concordia Publishing House, St. Louis, Missouri
Concordia Publishing House Ltd., London, E. C. 1

Library of Congress Catalog Card No. 67-24875
MANUFACTURED IN THE UNITED STATES OF AMERICA

Editor's Foreword

This book is one of a series of six in the Concordia Sex Education Series. It is written especially for pastors, teachers, youth workers and leaders, and all who are involved in parish planning programs, whether they are the Christian Education Committee or the leaders of organizations.

The other five books in the series are tools to help parishes that have become so motivated to move forward in the promotion of Christian sex education. They are: *I Wonder, I Wonder,* by Marguerite Kurth Frey, for kindergarten through grade 3; *Wonderfully Made,* by Ruth Stevenson Hummel, for grades 4 through 6; *Take the High Road,* by August J. Bueltmann, for junior high; *Life Can Be Sexual,* by Elmer N. Witt, for high school; and *Parents Guide to Christian Conversation About Sex,* by Erwin J. Kolb. Color filmstrips and records are available for the first three books in the series and for the *Parents Guide.*

This series of books is concerned with much more than merely imparting the biological facts of reproduction. There are many such books, and good ones, on the market. Furthermore, young people today are acquiring a good deal of knowledge through science courses.

Evidences all about us of increasing permissiveness, the search for a "new morality," and increasing high school marriages indicate that the knowledge of biological facts is very different from the development of Christian attitudes. There is a need to move into the confusion of our generation with positive help.

For too long the church has remained silent. In its broader sense, sex education is a part of Christian living. No person lives out his life in the neuter gender. He does so always as a man or as a woman, with all the drives, needs, and characteristics of men and women. If the church is going to help people develop in their Christian life, it needs to help them fulfill their roles as men and women. The church needs to be concerned with helping people of all age levels — young boys and girls, teen-agers, those preparing for marriage, young married couples, middle-aged couples, and aged people — to understand their roles as Christian men and women and to handle their sexuality with Christian responsibility.

This book is placed in your hands to help you carry out this task.

The author brings with his facile pen a good background for this book. He has a strong educational background, having served as teacher and administrator in Christian elementary schools as well as in the public school system. More recently he has served as executive secretary of education and youth for the Central Illinois District of The Lutheran Church — Missouri Synod. Currently he is associate executive secretary of schools for the Board of Parish Education in St. Louis, Mo.

Special thanks are due the editorial committee that assisted in planning this series: E. H. Ruprecht of Immanuel School, Valparaiso, Ind.; Frederick Nohl of the Board of Parish Education, St. Louis, Mo.; and Walter A. Juergensen of Concordia Teachers College, Seward, Nebr.

W. J. Fields

Contents

1

A Cry for Help

More than we like to admit, church families are having husband-wife and child-parent conflicts. Family friction is hurting children, embittering husband-wife relationships, and robbing homes of the love and forgiveness that ought to characterize the Christian home. Outward appearances are kept up. Inwardly there is anxiety and hurt, resentment and bitterness, loneliness and crying. Often this crying is an appeal for help — a crying that may not be heard because there is no one to listen or to help.

1

A CRY FOR HELP

We are involved in a vital matter. The objects of our special concern are the families in our own church and community. Some of these families of concern are pleading for help, but others are too modest or ashamed to ask for aid because their problems seem too delicate.

Whether the pleadings of these troubled families become audible or remain choked down in anxious silence, they are pleas that deserve a hearing. Answers ought to be given. Help must be offered. Every pastor, every counselor, every youth director is involved. The church is involved.

More than we like to admit, church families are having husband-wife and child-parent conflicts. Family friction is hurting children, embittering husband-wife relationships, and robbing homes of the love and forgiveness that ought to characterize the Christian home. Outward appearances are kept up. Inwardly there is anxiety and hurt, resentment and bitterness, loneliness and crying. Often this crying is an appeal for help — a crying that may not be heard because there is no one to listen or to help.

So few will listen or help, because so few care or understand or even care to understand.

The underlying conflicts and tensions are often sex related. Buried deep under surface signals lie the cancerous roots that feed on misinformed, misdirected, and unloving attitudes toward self, sex, and other persons. It is difficult for people with such problems to acknowledge, understand, or even speak of their problems. It is difficult to ask for help.

In recent years sociologists have made public startling findings on the sex attitudes and practices of modern men and women. The American public was taken a bit by surprise. Many people were downright shocked. Church leaders as well as research specialists found themselves discrediting those who conducted the surveys, criticizing the methods used in gathering the appalling statistics, and questioning the validity of their conclusions. Many of us didn't want to believe, and many didn't. Some were hopeful that in their much sampling the sociologists had somehow overlooked church families. We still wanted to believe that families that pray together, worship regularly, participate in parish activities, and apparently conform to an acceptable code of conduct have no such problems.

Then church groups, too, became interested in investigating the sex conduct and attitudes of church people in particular. Surveys were conducted, and statistics began to pile up. It was soon discovered that also church families have problems — serious problems growing out of unloving attitudes toward self and sex.

Early in the 1960s, at the North American Conference on Church and Family, social scientists reported their findings on sex-related problems. Their reports discussed premarital pregnancies, interfaith marriages, divorce and broken homes, the free sex attitudes of teen-agers, illegitimacy, infidelity, homosexuality, abortion, and related problems. The greatest concern expressed by the sociologists was that Americans have lost a stable moral standard. The "new morality" which suggests that behavior should be determined by the circumstances or situation in which a person finds himself, is an inadequate moral standard for the Christian person.

Few, if any, have escaped the influences undermining stable moral standards. Children, parents, youth — all are constantly being bombarded by sex stimuli that require responses. Many are responding haphazardly. Only some are asking for guidance in making correct and adequate decisions.

Judge or Counselor

Cal Moore had now been married 2 years. Things were not going well. Cal sensed that it was his own fault. He was irritable and hard to get along with. He felt guilty. Indeed, he felt it was wrong for him to continue having intimate relations with his wife.

Cal wanted help, but he hesitated to expose the problem. Something like this would not be easy to talk over. He knew that others in his church had talked to Pastor Williams about their private problems. He was encouraged.

Pastor Williams sensed that Cal's visit was not as casual as Cal had put on. The pastor's comments and questions helped Cal feel somewhat at ease. He became more talkative. He felt a sense of relief as he recalled and told experiences of childhood and youth. There was no judgment in Pastor Williams' voice or attitude. Cal continued:

"As a teen-ager I was caught — " It wasn't easy to say.

Pastor Williams sensed what Cal wanted to say and helped him along. Cal had been caught masturbating.

Cal's parents were shocked, disappointed, and determined that something had to be done immediately. The pastor could handle this matter. After all, Cal was attending the pastor's instruction class.

The pastor listened briefly. Then Cal listened. No Christian young boy would ever do a thing like this. What would Christ think? Did Cal realize that he had hurt his father and mother very, very much? Cal agreed.

Cal continued to listen as the pastor informed him of the serious consequences were he to continue the habit. Finally the pastor thought Cal was ready to make a promise — a promise never again to disgrace his body in such a shameful way. Cal promised. He meant to keep that promise.

But he didn't. He tried, but he couldn't.

The more he tried, the worse it became. He began to worry and to feel ashamed. Why wasn't he like the other boys his age? He felt guilty, ill at ease, and out of place.

He wanted to talk to someone about it, but there was no one who would understand. He couldn't go to his parents or pastor, because he would have to admit that he had broken his promise. He didn't want to hurt them again. He didn't talk it over with anyone — except himself, over and over and over again.

But now Pastor Williams was listening.

Now it was Pastor Williams' turn. Simply and briefly he helped Cal understand. Masturbation is a problem for most normal boys. In a way it is a sign that they are growing up and getting ready for manhood. To the best of the pastor's knowledge, no serious physical consequences result from masturbation. But the consequent sense of shame and guilt can be damaging. What Cal had done was wrong. Had Cal forgotten? Christ died for these sins — all of them. If God forgave Cal, Cal could forgive himself.

Both Pastor Williams and Cal knew that this wasn't a closed case. It would take time for Cal to understand all this, to change old habits and attitudes, and then to feel at home in this new perspective. But Cal was on his way.

At this point we cannot but ask whether Cal's life could have been different if his parents had had the advantage of some program of Christian sex instruction. What would have happened if they had had the opportunity to read the following from *Parents Guide to Christian Conversation About Sex,* one of the volumes in this sex education series?

> "There is no easy answer for what parents should do if they discover a child masturbating at this age, because many boys and some girls masturbate as a part of their experimentation and growth in searching for an expression of their sex urge. However, 'some medical authorities now regard masturbation as a step in preparation for adult sexual feelings. . . .' "
>
> Some people use the motive of fear and guilt to try to control the habit of masturbation, pointing out how God will punish it. But this is certainly not the Christian approach. Neither is it very successful. Most young people want to control the habit, for it is often accompanied by a sense of shame and guilt. . . .
>
> Christian parents ought to use the love of God as motive rather than fear of His punishment. When Christ lives in us, we have His power to help us control our lives. Understanding that it may be some lack in the teen-ager's life that causes him to masturbate, parents may help by guiding him in finding friends and companions, discovering ways of obtaining satisfaction from activities he enjoys, assuring him of their genuine love, or doing things with the family and with others.

Tom or Sharon?

Miss Langdon, teacher at Wilson Junior High, was counseling with Tom. Tom had excessive energy. Now and then Tom used poor judgment in choosing the time and place to "let go." Miss Langdon was determined that Tom could be subdued. Six months passed without improvement. Tom was becoming convinced that he was just a bad boy. In a routine check the school nurse's observations encouraged her to recommend that Tom have a physical examination. The doctor found that Tom was physically ill, and he proceeded to prescribe medication. It wasn't long before he was well.

During this same period of time Miss Langdon was unaware of Sharon's problem. Sharon was in the same homeroom with Tom; she was earning exceptionally good grades and was an example of perfect conduct. The teacher had ignored the fact that Sharon had no friends — that she did not seem to care for children her own age. Miss Langdon insisted that it was Sharon's maturity that caused her to seek companionship among members of the staff. Sharon's frequent absences and complaints of having "such an awful headache!" came to the attention of the school counselor. The counselor visited Sharon's home. During the weeks that followed, Sharon's story was pieced together. Sharon had been born out of wedlock while her mother was in high school. While Sharon did not know this, she did know that high school boys and girls were bad people. She knew it because her mother had told her — many, many times. Sharon had become a victim of distortion and prejudice.

Getting Ready to Help

"The church should intervene to break the circles of circumstances which keep producing sexually mixed-up people with sexually mixed-up kids who become parents of more sexually inadequate people." This comment from one of the participants of the North American Conference on Church and Family puts the problem of our concern in sharp focus.

Assuming first that the church must be concerned and second that the church wants to accept the challenge, we ask the following question: Is the church equipped to accept this challenge? With this question we invite the reader into our conversation. We know there are church workers — pastors, counselors, teachers — who are concerned, who have accepted the challenge, and who are equipping themselves for this ministry.

At a youth leaders' workshop I recently had occasion to relate the story of Cal and of Sharon. One of the pastors in attendance commented that Cal's teen-age experience had set the stage for distortion and future conflict. "However," he added, "I can't be too critical of Cal's first pastor." "You see," he added, "I probably would have counseled with Cal in the same way."

Another participant in the workshop, a teacher, confessed, "I hate to admit this, but I'm afraid there are many of us just like Miss Langdon."

If the church is to intervene "to break the circles of circumstances which keep producing sexually mixed-up people," it must prepare itself.

Is the church ready for the task? Pastor Williams is ready. No doubt countless others are ready. Many others are getting ready.

For many this will not be easy. For many it will mean breaking out of the circles of circumstances first for themselves, for they too have been caught by the chain of circumstances which we are intending to break.

A survey conducted within the United States by the Lutheran Churches reveals that few pastors or members have received sex instruction. Those having had sex instruction, revealed that the church's role seemed to be quite negligible. While there is complete agreement among lay people and pastors, according to the survey, that frank and sober discussion of sex should take place between parents and their children, only a third of them have had such conversations within their homes. As for enjoyment of sex in marriage but apart from procreation, the survey concludes that the figures reflect somewhat the general uncertainty growing out of variant teachings in the church through the centuries.

Where do we begin?

We begin with encouragement. In the survey just mentioned, 93 percent of the pastors and laity favored the idea of sex education. There was complete agreement between pastors and church members supporting frank and sober discussion of sex within the home.

Another note of encouragement is offered by W. Gordon Smedsrud, reporting insights from Lutheran Youth Research in a booklet entitled *What Youth Are Thinking*. He states: "Nearly every Lutheran high schooler interviewed wants 'instruction on Christian views of sex, courtship, and marriage' from the church. Almost 90% of them want help from the sacristy in what to look for in a life companion long before they come to that sacristy to arrange their wedding plans."

A final word of encouragement: in our concern we are encouraged by a gracious, loving, and forgiving God who is no less concerned. He assures us that His love remains certain, warm, and inviting. The Savior's attitude has not changed. His invitation still stands: "Come, you are Mine. I have redeemed you. I love you." And the Spirit of God continues to give assurance that man in Christ is a new creature.

God's love continues to be a love for the world of all kinds of people. Not only the middle class, not only a given age group, not just the moderate sinner, not only the acceptable conformist, but all are loved by the God who created them. All people — the poor and the rich, harlots, bank robbers and bank presidents, teachers and pupils, pastors and parishioners, gamblers and misers, teen-agers and the aged — all people need the love of God.

In the belief that many who participated in this survey are sincere in their request for help from the church, the Board of Parish Education of The Lutheran Church — Missouri Synod determined to provide this series of books on sex education. The volume you have in hand is an attempt to demonstrate the need for Christian sex education and to establish a point of view that is related to the church's task of proclaiming the Gospel.

2

The Church Must Speak

As the swift cultural changes have cut people adrift from their moorings, so many have also been cut adrift from their spiritual roots. Sources of spiritual power and influence have not always been available to them in a meaningful way. Many that have been cut adrift are at sea, just waiting to be rescued. They are lost and can't find their way home.

2

THE CHURCH MUST SPEAK

If the individual does not recognize that he is an object of God's creating love and that his life has purpose in God's design, he will not be able to know the right view of his sexuality. It is significant to note that as individuals lose sight of the divine dimension of life, they also lose perspective on sex, which is subject to so many secular distortions.

The reader whose interest and concern have led him this far may wish to pause here for a moment's reflection. Is sex education really a concern of the church? Isn't it rather the task of the social scientist, the educator, or the man of medicine? Viewing the vast amount of sex education literature for people of all ages, need I be involved and concerned?

If it is true that people who lose sight of the purpose of life also lose proper perspective on sexuality, then perhaps we can conclude that if people are to learn the correct view of sex, they must learn it from those whose ministry it is to spell out God's will for man's life. If the moral picture of our civilization is to be changed, the church must change it.

The church has been silent too long. It must cease rendering judgments and pious pronouncements upon its own people. This is not education.

We have deplored the damaging impact of sex stimuli upon our people. Too often the church has seemed little more than a refuge center for victims who come already twisted and broken. In too many cases the victims have found it not a refuge center but a judgment hall.

But these are the people who, with an almost unanimous plea, are asking for help — from the church. And as they ask, they too sense that from their twisted-and-brokenness has come a distorted view of life.

The Church Must Speak — Because in the United States:

One of every six brides is pregnant at the time of her wedding.

Every sixth bride and groom united in wedlock "until death do us part" will be separated by legal divorce action.

Two children per divorce will be robbed of their rightful heritage of parents who will love them, train them, and care for them.

Over 20 percent of the husbands and wives in the United States are guilty of infidelity.

Several hundred thousand illegally induced abortions occur each year.

Large segments of the male population are or have been involved in homosexual activities. Lesbianism among women is increasing.

The upswing in illegitimacy continues.

An increasing number of young, immature, unprepared, and often confused teen-agers are appearing at marriage altars to make life promises that they are incapable of keeping. (Chances of teen-age marriages ending in divorce are three and one-half times greater than in the case of their older counterparts.)

The church must speak because God's purpose in sex is being thwarted, and His intended blessings are falling as curses on countless American families.

Because of the Sentner Family

Jack Sentner and Lois Blair met in Chicago at a company convention. It was love from the very first. Jack from the Midwest and Lois from New York found it difficult to be together very often. Now and then they met for a weekend in Chicago. It was a quick courtship and a hurried wedding. They met their future in-laws the day before the wedding. Everyone was excited and thrilled about this love-at-first-sight romance.

The first months of married life were wonderful. It was Lois who first noticed the now-and-then coolness between them. Jack wanted to continue the "party"; Lois was more interested in her home. Differences of opinion were frequent. Tension rose. They hardly knew each other and Jack didn't want to talk about it.

When Jack, Jr., was born, Lois was sure that everything would be all right. Things were going much better — for a while. When Lois announced the prospect of another baby, Jack was furious.

Certainly the church has something to say to Jack and Lois. It should have said something a long time ago. And the children? Father and mother can hardly give their children a heritage they themselves do not possess.

Because of Kurt and Ruth

Kurt and Ruth had gone steady during most of their senior high year. Now they were graduated with little to do during the summer months. They were together more than ever.

Both had dated all through high school. Most of that time they were going steady with someone. Kurt's parents were proud that Kurt was popular, and Ruth's parents were thrilled that Ruth wasn't a wallflower — like the neighbor girl.

A summer vacation with nothing to do sounded like a lot of fun to Kurt and Ruth. Somehow, however, things were just not working out as they had hoped. Even before graduation most dates ended with intense necking sessions, but then there were other things happening to divert their attention. Now, however, they found themselves losing control, experimenting — everything but "going too far."

Perhaps this was to be expected. After all, each had had four years of dating experience. Each year dating had become a more exciting and intimate affair. This was to be expected. But Kurt and Ruth weren't happy about it. They were obsessed with each other. They were losing respect for each other and themselves, particularly as they continued to break the promises they made to each other.

What should they do? They talked about it. They couldn't get married because their parents would not stand for that. Ruth, and Kurt too, wanted to go to college. Why didn't they do what a lot of kids were doing? They could be careful. No one would find out. As long as they would get married someday, what difference would it make?

The church needs to speak because there are a lot of Kurts and Ruths who need to listen. And they have parents who need to listen.

Because of Jean and Al

When Al proposed to Jean, she was thrilled. But she wasn't quite sure. Should she accept? Al was quite different from her. He was as her parents had said, "worldly." Jean had often thought of herself as being on the "outside," mainly because her parents were a bit old-fashioned. Jean was 22, and this was her first proposal. She had always worried about being an old maid.

They were married. Al has changed and keeps telling the "fellas" he'd do it all over again. One thing is beginning to bother him more and more though — and Jean too. Al feels that they should wait before they begin their family. Jean agrees in a way, but feels that if they are going to postpone having a family, they should also discontinue having regular intimate relationships. To Jean sexual intercourse is wrong except when a family is being planned.

Jean and Al love and respect each other very much. But they have a problem.

The church must speak to help the Jeans and Als in communities all over the United States.

In Confusion

Children today are being born into a culture and social pattern quite unlike any previous generation. The population boom, social mobility, suburban living, the transition of formerly stable rural and semirural communities, the emerging new roles for male and female, the development and use of communication media, the free expression of literature and the arts, and the availability of the automobile have brought a new way of life.

All this has made an impression on young people too. It is not as easy today to control and direct the influences which affect the lives of young people as it was a generation ago. Young people are learning from their contemporaries rather than from parents and elders. Confusing ideologies, the "new morality," and exciting ways of life are giving them the "come on." Young people are being caught in currents of change. Centered in these swift currents is a turbulence over sex. Romantic, erotic love has become a new "it" in the lives of people — young people particularly.

A new dimension has been added as *the* prerequisite for marriage — romantic, erotic, idealistic love. Often this new dimension has displaced or replaced the former requirements. A new standard for this new emphasis on love has been established by the combined impact of the screen, the novel, or the TV set, which in the lives of many youth is more natural and realistic than any other standard or lack of one. Where Jack and Lois formerly were fashioned by stable and secure family paterns, community mores, and religious beliefs and practices, their modern counterparts are less and less the children of their homes, churches, and communities but more and more the products of the daily impacts of their contemporaries, music, art, literature, highly technical and emotionally structured communication media, and highy skilled admen.

Bert Loudin is a handsome and rather typical high school senior. He has his share of dates. The gang envies Bert his datebook filled with the names of the best-looking girls in town. Bert's "taste" is reflected in the array of pinups mounted inside his hallway locker. His somewhat disorganized notebook almost always contains a current movie or TV photo magazine. In spite of his parents' discouragements, Bert spends much of his time with girls and "thinking" about them.

Lora, a junior, wants to quit school. Ever since she was in seventh grade, she has been dating boys. She's always been attractive to boys. Her parents, particularly her mother, saw to it that Lora always had the right kind of clothes. Most of the time Lora had a steady. Having a steady was more important than anything else in the world. The first months of her junior year Lora began to put on extra pounds, and her clear complexion developed acne that cosmetics could not conceal. The regular set of boys started to avoid her. Now and then she dated some who weren't so nice. Then even they quit paying attention to her. Lora was crushed — and so were her parents. Lora just couldn't bear to go to school any longer.

In many respects Lora and Bert are typical teen-agers. Both had some sex education in school. What they didn't learn about sex at school they picked up from friends and reading material found here and there. Neither received much help at home. Bert frequently was warned not to stay out too late. Lora's mother was always ready to give opinions on dress and grooming.

Perhaps both Lora and Bert would have profited from a reading of August J. Bueltmann's *Take the High Road*. We quote from his chapter on "A Pleasing Personality for the High Road":

> If most of the favorable personality characteristics sound suspiciously like Christian virtues, it is because they are. The virtues a Christian seeks to cultivate are at the same time those peronality characteristics that make a person well liked. For example, Jesus

talked a great deal about self-denial. Some folks think He meant skipping food and fun. That isn't true. He meant conquering one's self — overcoming selfishness and self-centeredness, putting others first. Real popularity means self-denial. It means thinking first of the welfare and wishes of others. . . .

Love is not only the secret of popularity; it is the secret of happiness in life. It is one of the keynotes of the life in Christ. It is the way of acquiring a pleasing personality for the high road.

Through the Back Door

Since the beginning of this century the population of the United States has doubled. At the turn of the century more than 40 percent of the country's population lived on farms; more recent figures indicate a rural population of little more than 10 percent of the total. In 1900 the average life expectancy was less than 50 years; now it is over 70 years.

Inner-city commissions, urban renewal projects, tollways and freeways, rural life institutes, consolidated schools, suburbia — these are the terms by which we know the changes that have occurred and the adjustments, gross and fine, that have to be made.

Changes came quickly. Adjustments were hard to make. The ensuing problems mushroomed so quickly that many were hardly recognized till they were in full agony.

The sex revolution came in the back door. No one planned it that way.

Mr. Smith sold his business in a small Midwest village. Now he's one of the hurrying commuters catching the morning 7:20 and the afternoon 5:10. He didn't realize that he'd have so little time left for his family, what with church and civic activities, etc. He did take time to join the antismut campaign. He visited over a dozen newsstands, urging the peddlers to sweep the "filth" from their shelves. But in his haste at home he overlooked his son Bud studying the "nearly nudes" lounging in the magazines that always cluttered the Smith living room. It was Bud who suggested that looking at this kind of pictures made masturbating more fun. More and more, Bud was having trouble being a 13-year-old young man. He knew how to do housework, but he wasn't very good at doing things boys like to do. He even quit swimming lessons. He didn't like his teacher, Mrs. Drake.

Most of the parents of Central Community High School were pleased when they read the announcement that a course in sex education was being added to the curriculum.

"Maybe this will put a stop to some of the boy-crazy notions our girl has," commented Mrs. Lord. Mr. Lord agreed.

Some weeks later Sue excitedly told her parents about the course: "Right now we're talking about the various ways to be lovable. It's a lot better than that awful geometry."

Later that evening Mrs. Lord expressed her delight in the way the new course was being handled. "Isn't it wonderful that our children are interested in learning to be lovable?"

Again Mr. Lord agreed, but somehow he felt a bit uncomfortable about it all. As he recalled, he had been taught to be loving, not lovable. There seemed to be a difference.

Almost overnight it happened. It happened to the Lords, the Smiths, to Jean and Al, to Kurt and Ruth, to Bud, to Sue — to a lot of us who suddenly found ourselves cut adrift from our moorings.

The old social, economic, family, and community controls, inadequate as they may have been, are gone and must be replaced.

The church must speak.

The Church Must Speak

As the swift cultural changes have cut people adrift from their moorings, so many have also been cut loose from their spiritual roots. Sources of spiritual power and influence have not always been available to them in a meaningful way.

Many who have been cut adrift remain at sea, waiting to be rescued. They are lost and can't find their way home.

People, people of all kinds, are asking for help — help from the church. The help must be basic and must be addressed to the problem sources.

The church must speak to the people that are cut from their moorings — to bring them back home. The church has the Word of God. This Word has the invitation, the direction, and the power to persuade acceptance. If wrong views of sex come from a wrong view of life, the church must speak of the right view of life. The church must speak because it has the Word of life.

3

Exploring Our Heritage

"That sex can be a gift of God, to be received with gratitude and enjoyed freely, is a truth too long forgotten, and sorely in need of revival."

— David R. Mace, ***Hebrew Marriage***

3

EXPLORING OUR HERITAGE

As the church prepares to provide leadership in sex education, it recognizes that the disorder in both sex conduct and sex attitudes has arisen from general uncertainty growing out of the church's variant teachings through the centuries. The church needs to know what it should say to a world preoccupied with sex and confused about it. The church needs to know what correct Christian sex attitudes are.

In an attempt to find these answers the church must first reexamine the confusion of what has been said previously. It is true, no doubt, that an underlying cause of the moral picture we view today stems from the lack of a concise moral standard. It is not altogether true that the church has not expressed itself, as some would accuse, but rather that its expressions have too often been unclear, faulty, or even unscriptural.

We need to examine the roots of our current thinking.

The church has always taught about sex. Its teachings, however, have changed from time to time. *Sex and the Church,* a 1961 publication of the Family Life Committee of The Lutheran Church — Missouri Synod, reviews these changes. A summary of them will help us see more clearly what our heritage really is.

Sex Is a Gift of God

We begin with the Old Testament. Here it is clear that sex was regarded as a gift from God. It was a gift not only for the utilitarian purpose of procreation; the gift was also intended to satisfy mankind's deepest needs and to afford him enjoyment. There was one basic restriction, as might be expected. Sexual desires should find satisfaction only within marriage. Adultery, fornication, prostitution, and the various sex perversions were forbidden. Note how openly and clearly the Old Testament speaks on matters of sex. Over and over again Old Testament references to sex give the reader the impression that sex need not be justified, explained, or excused. In effect the Old Testament says, "Sex is good. It is a gift of God."

David R. Mace, author of an extensive work on marriage customs in the Old Testament, reveals an interesting insight. He says:

> The entire positive attitude to sex which the Hebrews adopted was to me an unexpected discovery. It is true that I had always been struck by the unembarrassed plainness of speech with which they discussed sexual matters. But I had not fully realized that it had its roots in an essentially "clean" conception of the essential goodness of the sexual function. This is something very difficult for us to grasp, reared as we have been in a tradition which has produced in many minds the rooted idea that sex is essentially sinful. That sex can be a gift of God, to be received with gratitude and enjoyed freely, is a truth too long forgotten, and sorely in need of revival.

For many of us this may seem to be an overstatement. It was for this writer. Repeated and unbiased cursory glances at the Old Testament convinced this writer of the truth of Mace's statement. The open and free manner in which the Old Testament speaks of sex was an unexpected discovery. It is hoped that the next few pages will help the reader make this same discovery.

It is true that the Old Testament places restrictions on the enjoyment of sex even within marriage. How do we explain these restrictions? First of all, they must be understood in the light of the entire positive attitude of the Old Testament toward sex. Frequently these restrictive regulations were not part of the Moral Law. Often they were part of the civil or the ceremonial ordinances under which the Hebrew people lived. For example, before giving the Law at Mount Sinai God prepared His people by telling them to wash and to have no sexual relations (Ex. 19:15). Again, David's men were not permitted to eat hallowed bread at Nob until Ahimelech had assurance that they had had no relations with women (1 Sam. 21:4). In both instances it would be unjustified, particularly in the light of other positive statements of the Old Testament, to conclude that therefore sexual relations were wrong. Sexual abstinence, like fasting, was prescribed as part of the preparation for worship.

Sexual abstinence during menstrual periods and before and after childbirth were part of the hygienic regulations followed by the Hebrew people. These restrictions, if for no other reason, were essential because sanitation practices and facilities were primitive.

Perhaps a few references are necessary to support the contention that the Old Testament speaks of sex in a positive and favorable light. Gen. 1:27 tells us: "Male and female created He them." When God surveyed all that He had made, it was with complete approval; "it was very good," including all the sexual beings.

The pleasure of sex, particularly as it is related to the joy of having children, is expressed frequently in the Old Testament without condemnation. Eve, we are told, "desired" her husband. In her old age Sarah looked forward "with pleasure" to having a child. Gen. 26:8 speaks of Isaac "sporting" with Rebecca in such a way that Abimelech knew that they were husband and wife. Early in the history of Israel, when polygamy was apparently tolerated, Ex. 21:10 stipulated that a wife was to be given her due "marital rights." Approval of sexual pleasure is implied in the regulation of Deut. 24:5. According to this regulation a new groom was exempt from military service for one year so that he might "cheer up his wife which he hath taken."

The positive attitude of the Old Testament toward sex is established when God describes His relationship to the Hebrew people. God tells of His love for His people by comparing it to the relationship of a husband and wife — the beautiful attraction that binds husband and wife together. The representation of Christ as the Bridegroom and of the church as the bride is a favorite allegory used in the Bible. The Song of Solomon, describing the love of the Lord for His church, does so in the bridal love of Solomon and Shulamite.

One can hardly imagine that the Lord would speak of His love for His people and His church in terms of a relationship that is essentially sinful, unholy, and unclean. Nor would the Lord speak in such terms and comparisons if He did not have the assurance that His listeners understood the terms in which He spoke.

Sex Is Good — New Testament

The New Testament reinforces the positive attitudes and conclusions of the Old. In speaking to the Greek and Roman world on the purpose of sex and its proper use within the marriage relationship, the New Testament concludes that sex is good.

Perhaps it is more than coincidence that the Lord chose the Cana wedding celebration as the occasion for His first miracle (John 2:1-11). At the feast He expressed more than a merely tolerant attitude toward marriage and the wedding festivities. Indeed, He applied His power to add to the joy and merriment of the occasion, turning water into a generous supply of excellent wine.

Again, it is more than coincidence that Christ used the wedding feast as the setting for two parables, the Foolish and Wise Maidens (Matt. 25:1-13) and the Marriage Feast. (22:1-14)

Jesus spoke His opinion clearly when He was questioned by the Pharisees, who tested Him with their query concerning the lawfulness of divorce (Matt. 19:3). Jesus simply stated that God created people male and female and for that reason men and women should marry and become one flesh. "What therefore God has joined together, let no man put asunder." (19:6)

It is Paul who once more stresses the relationship of spouses to each other to illustrate the relationship of Christ and His church. With this in mind he gives to husbands the encouragement that they should love their wives as Christ loved the church and gave Himself for it. For the wives He has the encouragement that they should submit to their husband's love as the church submits to the Savior's love. And finally we remember Paul's words to Timothy: "For everything created by God is good, and nothing is to be rejected if it is received with thanksgiving; for then it is consecrated by the Word of God and prayer." (1 Tim. 4:4)

Virginity and Celibacy Exalted — Church Fathers

We leave the New Testament era. We note a distinct change and trend in the attitude toward sex and marriage. Historians of that time note not only the change in attitudes but also the changes in practices with respect to marriage and family life. How can we explain this change of attitude? Historians note the moral corruption of the pagan world of the early centuries. The reaction of the early Christians became defensive and extreme. In their defense they quoted Paul out of context "It is well for a man not to touch a woman" (1 Cor. 7:1). This defense of the early Christians against pagan wickedness marked the entrance of negative attitudes toward sex and married life within the church. This attitude of the church, along with the current philosophical Greek thought of the period, made a lasting impact, which was to be a negative influence for generations to come.

We need to note here the influence of Greek philosophy in these early centuries. Greek thought made a sharp distinction between the soul and the body. The soul was associated with all that was good and divine; and the body with the source of all evil. Added to the developing distortions of the time were the teachings and practices of ascetic cults and mystery religions. More and more general acceptance was given to the thought that all sexual activity, even within a legitimate union, was stigmatized as inherently evil. Out of this kind of thinking grew the opinion that virginity and celibacy were far more God-pleasing than marriage.

We need to explore our heritage a bit further. Let's examine the period of the apostles and the postapostolic fathers.

The authors of *Sex and the Church* report comprehensively on their findings of this period. Note the development of distortion as the thinking of several of the church fathers is summarized:

Clement of Alexandria: Marriage is sacred. It is to be kept pure from all things that would defile it.

Justin Martyr: Marriage is only for the purpose of procreation. Christians must therefore exercise self-control. Virginity, for both men and women, is highly desirable.

Origen: Adam did not have sexual knowledge of his wife till after the Fall. Had it not been for the Fall, the human race would very likely have been propagated in some mysterious or angelic manner, without sex and therefore without sin.

Chrysostom: God established marriage primarily for procreation. However, since the Fall the chief end of marriage is to be a remedy for concupiscence. Marriage is good, but virginity is better.

Jerome: It is not good that man should touch a woman. Therefore it is necessarily evil to do so. Marriage cannot be good because it renders prayer difficult. Those individuals who have become saints even though they were married, did so because they kept a virginal life even in their marriage.

Augustine: Virginity and self-denial are meritorious works and pathways to God. The suppression of sex life is a positive good.

We agree with the authors of *Sex and the Church* as they summarize this period, "One thing is certain: the warped thinking of this period shaped Christian thought for centuries to come."

Sex Is Second Best — Aquinas

The "warped thinking" of the first 10 centuries after Christ did influence Christian thought for centuries to come. We note this truth as we study the thought and practice of the Middle Ages. Here we find the church exalting virginity, refusing marriage to the clergy, and holding that marriage is more an institution than a personal relationship. The teachings of the scholastics during this period perhaps more than any other factor determined the teachings of the church concerning man's sexuality. We note the significance of these teachings as we study the scholastic philosophy as it was systematized by Thomas Aquinas.

Aquinas maintained that to live the good life is to live in accordance with right reason. This was in keeping with the classical tradition. It is through reason that man has communion with God. Aquinas contended that sex is good but that it is a second-rate good because of its interference with the placid contemplative life. Thomas Aquinas held that sex was a gift of God. Why? Because it was essential to procreation. After all, this was the only means of bringing souls into life. Aquinas further insisted that the thoughts of the heart were of utmost importance and that a married person might actually be better than a virgin if his inner attitudes toward sex were holier.

Aquinas approved of sexual relations within marriage. Whatever evil there might be in sexual activity within marriage is a punishment for original sin, and such evil is covered and excused by the marriage blessing. Accordingly, Aquinas suggested that the marriage act could be considered virtuous under two conditions: if it was performed (1) for the purpose of begetting children or (2) as a debt to the partner who might otherwise be driven to fornication. As one traces the history of sex attitudes and practices since the beginning of Christendom, he senses that much that had been said or thought earlier came to be embodied in the teaching of Thomas Aquinas. In Aquinas these thoughts were brought together in a unified philosophy of sex and marriage. Unfortunately, however, it was a philosophy that was in many ways out of step with Old and New Testament teaching.

Sex Is for Marriage — Luther

The Reformation marks the beginning of the church's change of attitude toward sex, marriage, and family. This is true, it should be noted, of both the Protestant and the Roman Catholic Church. The church's point of view, ofttimes revolutionary in nature, was expressed by the reformers of that day. Luther's views, developed over a period of years, point to and summarize the church's change in attitude.

Students of Luther recognize considerable variation in his teachings concerning sex and marriage. As his Biblical view of sin, redemption, and justification by faith become dominant in his theology, Luther's view on sex and marriage becomes modified and established. Luther did not consider the body sinful in itself. The devil, according to Luther, had spoiled the beautiful instinct of sex. The sex drive and desire is not sanctified merely by making marriage a sacrament. It is sanctified when people let God's grace in Christ hallow all the acts and transform them into deeds of faith, love, and service.

To Luther sex was as natural and necessary as hunger and thirst. He opposed celibacy because, as he said, vows cannot unsex a person. He did much to counteract the negative attitudes that had developed in the church during previous centuries. He did so when he insisted that it is faith that lifts marriage out of the purely physical realm and transforms even the trials of marriage into the arena of true Christian love. As Luther's theology developed, his concern for the total person became increasingly significant. To Luther the body and the soul were two sides of one life. The sexual side was not to be denied or repressed but properly used for God as God intended within the confines of marriage.

Puritans, Pietists, Rationalists

In surveying our heritage, we need to glance also at the expressions and attitudes dominant in the post-Reformation period. The curious blendings of the teachings of the Pietists, the Puritans, and the Rationalists of the early American scene have contributed in significant measure to the views that have dominated American attitudes on sexuality and human life. Here we note the influence of Calvin. His emphasis on obedience to the Moral Law was attractive to those who held that the moral life gives evidence and assurance of being in the state of grace. These teachings found great acceptance among the Pietists and the Puritans.

The Puritans, who prized moderation in all things, sought to regulate their behavior and practice according to what would be completely loyal to God. Complete loyalty requires complete obedience to God and takes precedence over all that is cherished by man. Among the Puritans such a sense of loyalty did not foster positive attitudes toward human sexuality.

The Pietists, who viewed Scriptures primarily as a mirror of holiness, shunned the pleasures of the world. Thus they offered proof to the world that they were regenerate. Even within marriage the pleasures of sex, they concluded, must involve sin.

The Rationalists substituted reason for the authority of Scripture. They refused to accept any standards except those established by nature, reason, and experience. This led to the acceptance of a humanistic morality. Chastity was regarded as superficial.

We have surveyed the more significant attitudes and trends of thought expressed during earlier centuries inside and outside the Christian church. These influences have come to be reflected in American life and thought today. They are part of the culture that influences us.

Understanding Our Inheritance

This, then, is our inheritance. Depending largely on our own family origins and environment, we may acknowledge one or the other view as dominant in our own thinking.

Perhaps here we have arrived at the first "So what?" in our considerations. Now we may suggest, on the basis of what has been said, several points of view or attitudes that need to be assumed by church workers.

The first point is that we who are working in Christian parishes should be keenly aware that the people in them have also received much the same mixed inheritance. Many have become victims of their culture. There will be those who continue strong adherence in views and in practice to the cultural patterns they have inherited. Others may find themselves challenging traditions that are a part of their family background. Some of them will have developed extremely liberal and nonconforming ways of life in reaction to their inherited tradition. Others will reject completely the family cultural pattern. Among them we are apt to find confusion, because in their rejection many fail to establish a point of view that can serve as a meaningful substitute.

We need to be concerned for still another reason. Although the lives of our parishioners have been filled with sex stimuli and talk of sex, few have had ample opportunity for conversation and education through which wholesome attitudes toward sex could be learned and established. Least of all has the church afforded them opportunity for such conversations in an atmosphere in which they might best take place. It is not surprising, then, that many people consider their sex life something entirely apart from their church and Christian life.

Because the heritage described above continues to prevail among many church members, we submit that any program of Christian sex education must be concerned with this heritage, overcoming its weaknesses by fostering better understanding and ethically sound points of view. The Concordia Sex Education Series addresses itself to this concern. In *Wonderfully Made: What Preteens Want to Know,* Mrs. Hummel writes as follows to her young readers:

> For you have been wonderfully made. Your Creator expects great things from you. As part of His loving plan, He created your sex and all that goes with it. Because of this gift, you will one day have the privilege of working with Him in the creation of new life. As a father or a mother, you will be able to create a happy home for your children. By your love and care you will be able to show them a little of what God's love is like.
>
> In the years to come you will be able to enrich the world in many ways. You are preparing for this future life even now, by growing up fully in mind and body, in feelings and abilities. At times you are beginning to taste the excitement of doing things for yourself and making friends on your own. In times of difficulty, you realize the comfort of having a family to fall back on. . . .
>
> Jesus, your Brother, knows all about the problems that growing up brings. He was once your age and He knows how it feels. Through His Spirit He is with you always. With His guidance you can decide for the right and the good in life. Following God's will always, you will be able to say, "It's good to be alive!"

Should all our concern be reserved for the people of our parish? Hardly, for we dare not neglect our personal needs. How have the traditions of the past shaped our own family culture? To what degree are our own attitudes and judgments on sexual matters based on traditional but questionable assumptions? We cannot assume that the tradition out of which we have come is necessarily correct in all respects, nor can we condemn outright those who come to us with differing opinions. As we work with our people to arrive at positive and wholesome concepts, we will have to take into account our own resistance to change and our natural reluctance to accept and adjust to newfound principles and beliefs. Two generations will have to move forward at once. If teachers and parents are to prepare children for adulthood in the present moral conflict, through study and discussion they themselves must come to some clearer understanding. Thus they will develop truly adequate views for themselves as they gain the knowledge and skills needed for guiding the younger generation.

It is obvious that if Christian people are to relate their sex and family life to Christian life, the church will have to offer guidance by setting forth Biblical, practical, and positive points of view on sex and marriage. The church dare not remain silent but must engage its people in conversation that will lead them into wholesome ways of thinking and living.

In this generation the church cannot afford to continue the silence and hypocrisy of the past, nor can it condone the promiscuity, licentiousness, and pornography of the present. It must teach explicitly the sinfulness of human nature, an authentically Christian view of sex, and willing submission to God's guidance in the Scriptures.

The church, entrusted as it is with the Gospel, needs to face realistically the current sex revolution and to give effective guidance with materials and methods for teaching not only children and youth but also adults. Certainly the church cannot give silent consent to the accelerating breakdown of morals so evident in our society. Rather it must raise its voice against fallacies and philosophies courting further deterioration. The church must do something even though some insist it should do nothing lest it usurp parental authority. If the church is to speak, we must bear in mind that for many it may seem novel or even strange for the church to address itself to the subject more openly and with candor. Many church people, too, will feel uneasy as they begin to speak on such intimate matters usually discussed — if at all — more privately, self-consciously, and with reserve approaching secretiveness. But conversation there must be in the context of the truth that God has given us to speak and live.

Sex is admittedly one of the basic human drives; yet it is but one of many facets of the Christian life. We cannot address ourselves to sexual life without speaking to the individual's total person and needs. Indeed, many of the frustrations experienced by individuals in their sexual life are manifestations of more basic problems in adjustment to life as a whole. A right view of sex begins with a right view of life, and a right view of life includes its sexual aspects.

Who am I? Why am I here? Who cares about me? These remain man's basic concerns and questions. The church has answers to these questions, and it should not hesitate to share them. As the individual grasps adequate answers to these basic questions, he comes to a fuller understanding of life. Within this setting we can begin to teach the right view of sex. As the individual recognizes that he is the yield of God's creative love and that life has significance and meaning in service to God and his fellowman, he comes to a fuller understanding also of his own sexuality.

4

What Should the Church Say?

Sex is God's idea, not man's. It is not by accident or miscalculation but by the deliberate design of God that sex pervades so much of created life. Sunfish and salmon, tigers and elephants, sparrows and robins, corn and wheat, pansies and goldilocks, elms and oaks — all possess sex designed and made by God. Sex is good. God says so in the very nature of His wonderfully complex creation.

4

WHAT SHOULD THE CHURCH SAY?

Sex Is Good

Some find this hard to believe. God made Adam. Adam was alone and lonely. God determined that this was not good, so He made Eve, a helper "fit for him." God made them to be "one flesh" and promised them children. Then God looked on His creation. It was good. He blessed Adam and Eve.

Sex is God's idea, not man's. It is not by accident or miscalculation but by the deliberate design of God that sex pervades so much of created life. Sunfish and salmon, tigers and elephants, sparrows and robins, corn and wheat, pansies and goldilocks, elms and oaks — all possess sex designed and made by God. Sex is good. God says so in the very nature of His wonderfully complex creation.

Louise Stranton had completed a freshman college course in preparation for marriage. Now she knew all the facts, she thought. She was ready for marriage. She had learned all about glands, hormones, chromosomes, about organs and their technical names and functions, about skills and techniques, about mating and dating and even intercourse. But this is not enough.

It is regrettable that so many brides and grooms enter marriage without adequate preparation. Facts are important. Thousands of pages have been written to tell the physical facts of sex and reproduction. But this is only part of the story.

The church can tell the whole story. The church must tell it because God is involved.

"I believe that God has made me . . ." still remains the Christian's confession. God has given me eyes, ears, fingers, feet, "and all my members" — my whole body. God did not create man and then withhold from him His creative power. His life-giving force is still at work in every rosebud and acorn, in every living creature. God continues to make men and women sexual beings with every force and power of His design.

"I will praise Thee, for I am fearfully and wonderfully made. Marvelous are Thy works, and that my soul knoweth right well" (Ps. 139:14). In *Take the High Road* the author speaks to teen-agers this way:

> God gave you the body you have. It is now up to you to take care of what you have been given. Suppose that your father gave you his gold wristwatch, saying: "Take care of this for me. Wear it, use it, and enjoy it. Later I'll ask for it back." What would you do with the watch? Would you crack walnuts with it? Would you toss it on the sidewalk to see how high it will bounce? Of course not! You would use it to tell the time of day. You would use it to tell others the time. Your heavenly Father has given you your body, more wonderful and valuable than the most expensive watch ever made. What will you do with it? You will take the best possible care of it, avoiding needless risks and using it as God intended. Why? Because your body really belongs to God. The apostle Paul wrote: "You do not belong to yourselves; you were bought at a price. Then honor God in your body." (1 Cor. 6:20 NEB)

Sex Is Still Good

"It takes some real hard believing to think of sex as anything but bad," said a teen-ager.

"What makes you say that?" asked the youth counselor.

"What's good about it? I mean the way we live nowadays."

Yes, that is the question: "What is good about sex?"

Let's go back — way back. God made man and woman, husband and wife. Theirs was a perfect love affair, a perfect marriage. Not only did they love each other; together they also loved God.

When God observed Adam's loneliness, He did not shape another man as a companion for him. He made a woman, Eve.

God made Adam and Eve a pair but different. Their differences were not just physical and organic. The man was male with male characteristics, and the woman was female with female characteristics. The distinctive characteristics of the one complemented those of the other. This is sex.

Together Adam and Eve loved God, and God loved the two of them.

The time came when Adam and Eve no longer loved God as they had. Sin separated them from Him. Their love turned in on themselves. By distortion of their love for each other, both became self-conscious and self-centered. Neither possessed the will, the strength, or the power to live in love and harmony with the other.

But God continued to love. He looked upon His fallen creatures and had compassion. His compassion came to their hopelessness with the promise, "My Son will be your Savior."

Fallen mankind came to be redeemed fully, not just partly. Through the saving activity of Jesus Christ, man came to be reunited with God as a whole being and a total person. God's love and redemption includes man's sexual nature. Mankind, in Christ, becomes a new creation. Through rebirth in Christ, man is again able to serve and love God and his fellowmen in joy.

As man loves and serves, he does not deny his sexuality but accepts and uses it according to his Creator's original intent. His entire life moves in the direction of spiritual maturation. This process involves within himself a constant struggle between good and evil also in his sex role. Within this struggle man is assured of sustained strength and power of the Spirit of God and the daily and constant forgiveness of sins. The new creature in Christ is able again to respect himself, to love God, to love humankind, and to love a spouse according to God's will and design.

Sex Is Important

The post-World War II years have been host to a sexual revolution. Sexual promiscuity and liberalism have overthrown sexual mores of previous generations as Puritanical and Victorian. We are constantly bombarded with the message that sex is vital and that sexual pleasure is the chief component of a rewarding life. The advertising media endeavor to sell everything from beverages to machinery with an appeal to the sex drive, and in the campaign they market a sex emphasis that sets off a chain reaction of views, behavior, and distortion.

In the light of what has been said, it might seem ridiculous for the church to advance any further claim supporting the importance of sex. But the church must speak of the real importance of sex.

Too often the church has, either by silence or by negative propositions, denied the essential goodness and importance of sex. This attitude has, some would argue, been one of the primary causes of the confusion and revolution that is taking place. Church members, teen-agers, married couples, single people, and adults have had a difficult time finding an acceptable moral code.

Some have espoused an attitude that virtually denies their sexuality. They have thus denied themselves a strength and blessing which God intended for them. Others have found themselves guilty of violating their sexual code with resultant pangs of conscience. Others have assumed an "enlightened" attitude, determined essentially by the societal norms and views. Some, particularly teen-agers, have revolted. We are living, they say, in a new age. Freedom in sex is part of this expression of this new age.

The church needs to speak of the importance of sex, if for no other reason than to refute any presumption that the church is opposed to sex. The church will have to clear the air of the erroneous assumptions with which it has been discredited. It can hope to negate the carnal sex emphasis growing out of the sex revolution and to establish a standard of sex life acceptable to Christian men and women.

Theologians in recent years are in general agreement concerning the basic purposes of sex. They suggest the following three: companionship, sex relations and procreation. Opinions differ concerning which of the three is primary. One writer suggests that this argument on priority should cease and acceptance be given to the unity and interrelation of these purposes within the total unity of marriage. Perhaps great harm has been done in the past by stressing one purpose and deemphasizing another. As we observe the relationship of all aspects of sexual life, we begin to comprehend its essential goodness and its importance. As we see the unified purpose of sex, we can observe the relationship of the full sex life reserved for marriage, for only within marriage can these purposes be accomplished and blessings bestowed.

Much of the confusion and apprehension concerning sexual expression springs from sources that deny sex as part of God's design and creation. God made human beings heterosexual; male and female are meant for each other and are to complement each other. Therefore the Christian man and woman accept sexuality within life as something important, good, sacred, and something to be honored. Man was created body and soul, redeemed body and soul, and is sanctified body and soul.

We must reject the many half-truths and errors that have crept into the thinking of the church through the years. The authors of *Sex and the Church,* in speaking of "A Christian Interpretation of

Sex," list the following half-truths and errors: (1) that sex per se is sin; (2) that sex sins are unforgivable or the worst sins in God's sight; (3) that the body is evil and its functions nasty; (4) that only things of the spirit or soul can be good; (5) that anything associated with the material things of the world is of itself evil and displeasing to God; (6) that all pleasures, particularly those derived from sex, are sin; (7) that the commandment against adultery is wholly negative, a prohibition without a positive side; (8) that in sinful man can be no right sexual desire; (9) that virginity is the only pure state; (10) that celibate life is holier than married life; (11) that such ascetic practices as continence in marriage help to earn the favor of God; (12) that the first sin was a sexual act, the eating of the fruit being a metaphor for it; (13) that Christianity is a matter of following regulations: do not handle, do not taste, do not touch (Col. 2:21); (14) that marriage merely legalizes sexual relations; (15) that sexual activity is animallike and unworthy of man; and (16) that sexual desire is one of the "lower instincts" of man.

These and similar half-truths or errors have led to confusion, uneasiness, and wrong attitudes. They have burdened consciences unnecessarily, thus spoiling many a marriage. Wherever the traditional view that sex is basically sinful has been taught or caught, it is obviously going to be difficult to put across the salutary truth that sex is and can be good.

Sex Is for Marriage

All people are sexual beings. Each individual is either man or woman, male or female. This sexuality, or state of being sexual, involves more than biological urges and sexual relationships. Sexual identity includes much more than anatomical structure, distinctive organs with distinctive functions. Social scientists have made significant contributions in analyzing and distinguishing the dominantly male and the dominantly female characteristics. It is interesting to note how in combination the male structures, features, and characteristics equip a man for his special role in life. The same is true of the female set that fits out a woman.

Human beings naturally need one another. Their needs are social, physical, psychological, and spiritual. Some of these needs are personal and grow out of being sexually male or female. The needs of the individual are met in interrelationships with other human beings. Because of the heterosexual nature of some of these needs, satisfaction for them is found in relationships with the other sex. Here the emphasis is on the sexes not as opposites but as complements.

According to God's design, human beings satisfy certain of their personal needs in heterosexual relationships. Marriage is the divine arrangement in which a man and a woman come together in a most intimate, personal, and dynamic relationship. Within marriage each spouse is to offer satisfaction and fulfillment and to find satisfaction and fulfillment. This is the unitive function of marriage.

According to God's design, another purpose and function of marriage is procreation. Within the bonds of love and unity a husband and his wife are to become father and mother, God's agents for bringing children into the world. Through love a family comes into being, creating an atmosphere of deep love in which the children are to be loved, nurtured, taught, and trained in God's way and will.

The unitive and procreative functions of sex in marriage cannot be dissociated. This is what the church must say. Who else can say it so well?

In this context the author of *Parents Guide to Christian Conversation About Sex* writes:

> "The opposite sex" is an unfortunate misnomer. When God made human beings as male and female, He did so not simply for the sake of variety, nor that they would be different or "opposite." He rather made the two a team — "male and female created He them" (Gen. 1:27). "I will make him a helper fit for him" (Gen. 2:18). Each was made a part of the completed whole. Alone neither fulfills the entire purpose of God's creative design. They complete each other as suitable helpers, as complementary parts of one intended unit. For this reason it is much more accurate to refer to the other sex as the "complementary sex" rather than the "opposite sex."
>
> This is apparent from the "built-in longing and desire" that the sexes have for each other. This need "penetrates into all phases of living." Men and women need each other socially, psychologically, and spiritually, as well as physically. Marriage merges these complementary needs, so that ideally each partner finds his needs fulfilled in the other. This is true also physically. In sexual relationship the husband and wife become "one flesh." The Bible uses the meaningful word "know" to describe the unique way in which the man and the woman become "one flesh" with each other. Here they reveal themselves and share a knowledge of themselves to each other that can be communicated in no other way.

The Christian lives under the constant divine encouragement that his whole life glorify his Creator. Any sexual relationship outside the framework that God has set is a mismating in which the participants cannot give glory and honor to their Maker. The meeting of two bodies cannot generate love. If nothing more than an incidental physical union exists between two people, very often the meeting of the bodies convinces of the shallowness and emptiness of the relationship, freezes out the romantic aspects of the act, and makes sexual expression distasteful and repulsive. Sex can only express a love that already exists. Only within the framework of God's design can the sexual act glorify the God who created male and female.

Christians know how Christ loved the church and how they are to love Christ and one another. Christian husbands and wives understand their love for each other in the context of divine love. Thus their love cannot be one of bondage and coercion but will be one of wonderful submission and willing commitment.

The Right View of Life

We are now ready for a kind of about-face. The church must speak of the goodness, importance, blessings, and purposes of sex. But this is not the church's primary message. The church's task is to teach the right view of life.

The church is not an agency of reform. It possesses a transforming power, and its business has to do with transformation. Whatever and whenever the church speaks of sex, it must do so in the context of its primary and essential message, with awareness that it is speaking a dynamic word that has transforming power.

As the church's central transforming message of the meaning of life — and death — takes root in the lives of people, and as right views of life are accepted, the church's expression on the Christian's sex life takes on meaning and finds responsive acceptance.

Let's be specific as to the central message and its transforming power.

The Essential Message — God Is

God does exist. He is real. He is almighty, powerful, full of compassion and love, Creator of all things, and active in the current affairs of men. This world is in His hands, and He will have His way with it. He will not be mocked. He is just, and His justice will prevail. All men will be called before Him to give account.

God is not just a pious expression, a vague and lofty idea, or a gimmick giver to a thing-loving world. He is more than a Sunday sentiment and a weekday ideal for men who are trying to make the grade by themselves.

This God is lovingly concerned how we live our lives as Christian males and females, as lovers, parents, and children. He has laid down rules and has promised blessings and punishments. He is concerned and will not be ignored. He is God, whom man can't change. He is a loving God. He bought us "with a price." We are His and not our own.

Christ Measured Up

Before this makes any sense, we have to speak of two realities, both of which are unpopular. If we claim adherence to Scripture, we cannot escape the term "sin" along with its definition and the statement of consequences. Man finds it difficult to talk of sin; it deflates his ego, the one thing he wants to build and preserve. His ego goes down for the count as soon as he admits the word *sin* into his vocabulary of life. But this is exactly what must happen if man is to speak of Christ.

If man wants to speak of the Christ who measured up, he has to face still another ego-deflating reality. Man does not and cannot measure up. Nothing man does or can do will move a just and demanding and very real God. This is an especially difficult admission for man who has broken open the 20th century. But it is an admission man must make if he is to speak of Christ.

Once man is willing to make these two admissions, the Christ who measured up has something to say to the man who can't measure up.

The Christ speaks first of judgment. In all justice the man who has declared his unfitness and pleaded his guilt has but one expectation — the judgment, condemnation, and payment in penalty for crimes committed. But to this man the Christ then speaks pardon with penalty paid — no judgment.

On the repentant harlot, on the prodigal who returns, the Christ pronounces no judgment.

In the zero hour of God's dealing with man stands a cross. On that cross the judgment was made and the penalties were paid. There God's wrath and justice made their claim. With that wooden measuring post behind Him the Christ, the God-man who rose again, announces: "The penalty has been paid. I have measured up. Because I have measured up, so have you."

To the penitent sinner, the involved and anxious teen-ager, the unfaithful and guilt-ridden spouse, the homosexual, the masturbator — to every repentant sex violator — the Christ who measured up now speaks the steady and certain assurance of no judgment.

To all who claim the name Christian and with that claim confess guilt and plead for mercy, the Christ speaks no judgment.

Then go, and sin no more. This is the second word of Christ.

The Christian man or woman who accepts the judgment and is declared innocent immediately becomes intimately and wonderfully involved with Christ. Christ's "sin no more" becomes directive and challenge, much more than a mere hope that soon proves empty, idealistic, unrealistic, and wishful.

Through the saving activity of Christ, man and woman enter a unique and meaningful relationship with Him who bought them for a price. Over and over again Paul speaks of the faithful as being "in Christ." By virtue of a God-bestowed faith, born-again people are members of His body, the church, of which Christ Himself is the Head.

People of God are people of love, living for Him and through Him, having one mind — the mind of Christ. The Christian life becomes a life of growth "to the measure of the stature of the fullness of Christ" (Eph. 4:13). This maturation is creative, always seeking improvement through change for the better.

When Christ gives the directive "sin no more," He gives assurance that in Him what He commands is possible, that "living in the Spirit, we walk by the Spirit." Christ is not the ideal that knocks us down in failure. He is man's Righteousness. Within this state of righteousness man's every word, thought, and deed — his eating, his drinking, his work and rest, his pleasure and loving — can and do glorify Him who is the Head, the Lord Christ.

This is the church's message of transformation. Within the context of this message the church's statements on sex have significance. Embodied in this message is the motive, the desire, and the power to live a proper sex life. From this message the transformed, born-anew person in Christ has the want-to and the how-to for living his sex life responsibly, enjoyably, and with intended blessing.

For Sinners

Sherwood Wirt, in his *Magnificent Promise,* tells of what reportedly happened in Edinburgh: A venerable old Scot seer was at the Communion table next to a young lady. As the elements were extended to the lady, the Scot noticed her back away hesitatingly with tears in her eyes. "Take it, lassie," he invited. "It's for sinners."

"It's for sinners." Let this thought serve as a backdrop to the concerns of the next few pages.

The church can be the best-equipped classroom for the teaching of the sex life. We are not suggesting that the church, which proclaims the Word of life on Sunday, needs merely to busy itself with teaching words of sex on Monday. We are saying that the Gospel, the Word of life, must always be proclaimed to the whole person, including his sexual nature. We are saying that sex education in the church classroom must always be related to the Gospel message, the Word of life.

The Wrong View of Life

Since many distorted views of sex grow out of distorted views of life, there is value in identifying the characteristics of the wrong view of life.

Let's explore this more fully. Let's look at the crowds around us. Let's look at people, particularly church members. Let's see if we can understand them.

Understanding people is not a simple matter. It is complicated because people are complicated.

At the outset let us be aware of the clue given us in 1 Sam. 16:7: "Man looketh on the outward appearance, but the Lord looketh on the heart." As we look at people, it is so easy for us to be duped by their outward appearances. It is easy to be concerned with people as they appear, rather than as they really are. And we might add, it is so much easier to apply soft salves to a surface wound than to reach the heart with a life cure.

If it were possible to see the heart of a person, we would see him as he really is — as God sees him. That person would stand before us stripped of all hypocrisy and pretense.

Fallen man does an excellent job of concealing his inner self, of covering up all he can of what he knows is wrong within.

He longs to achieve something and to be someone. He feels a profound need to prove his worth to all those around him, including God. When sin slipped into the world, man began the race to prove himself better than he is. Call it psychology or theology as you will, it remains true that sinful man is constantly striving to be what he was intended to be, a perfect and holy being.

Behavior reflects this drive to be something, to justify self, and to seem, if not to be, perfect. The sex offenses and misdeeds that have taken place in the name of establishing personhood are legion. This is true whether the offenses are overt and public or covert and private.

The drive to establish personhood sexually may take various directions within the same person. A teen-ager, driven by the pressure to prove himself to his peers, may participate in a sexual activity or a sex-related activity. To prove himself to his parents, his teachers, or the pastor, he may well assume another role. If he feels that he has failed on either front, he may engage in the secret sins of sex perversion or sex fantasy. Often these offenses are the resort of persons who have not, or feel they have not, succeeded in convincing others of their importance. The chronic masturbate is likely to be a person who has failed to be a real man in real life, so he seeks momentary compensation and retreat from the battle of proving himself in his real world. In *Life Can Be Sexual,* one of the books of this series, Elmer Witt says:

> The masturbation complex is the most serious dimension of the struggle of sex turned in upon oneself. This takes place when masturbation is used as a means of escape when the going gets tough. The escape pattern digs its own rut. And the habit can easily fix a person's sexual attitude at a level on which others are manipulated in fantasy to serve his satisfaction. This can make "sexual communication" as we have described it almost impossible.

Samuel was right. As we look at the crowds around us, we observe outward appearances. However timid or violent these appearances are, they are part of the proving and hiding process. Suffice it to say, there is little value in treating the appearances and ignoring the ulcerated heart. Let's say it again: the church is the best-equipped classroom for sex education because it does not have to be content with superficial treatments. The church has medication for the heart.

Morality or Purity?

Let's examine another phase of the wrong view of life. We have reference to the concept implied in the term "morality." It's a high-sounding word that appeals to the best in man. It almost sounds religious. We have no quarrel with the idea or ideal of morality or of moral goodness. But the popular concept of morality has potential for misdirecting the unsuspecting Christian.

Man speaks of morality. God speaks of purity. We need to know the difference. Morality is relative to time, place, and community culture. Morality is virtue widely regarded as within man's natural potential. Purity, on the other hand, is an absolute determined by God, who permits no variance, no tolerance. Purity is not attainable by man; it is something God gives.

"Blessed are the pure in heart," says the Lord, "for they shall see God." It is easy to take these words as an inducement to achieve perfect morality. But this the words do not imply. God here says to each sinner, "Accept my forgiveness in Christ; you will have a pure heart; you will see Me."

The tension between the concepts of morality and purity adds a weighty dimension to the goal and method of sex education. The church can speak of this tension because it carefully distinguishes between morality and purity and is concerned with purity beyond morality. Because it can speak God's forgiveness in Christ, the church can point to purity as a goal that by God's grace can be realized.

The Scottish divine referred to earlier had the right idea. Perhaps the confidence he expressed in the grace and mercy of God is not shared by as many church leaders as we might think. In too many circles it seems that the achievement of moral perfection is prerequisite to making an effective appeal to the grace and mercy of God. How often does the church leave the impression that the unmarried but pregnant teen-ager, the cheating husband, or the flighty divorcee must first make amends and set the crooked straight before approaching the mercy seat of a forgiving God? Of the harlot, we might recall, Jesus first required repentance, not reparations.

Since the goal is not conformation (morality) but transformation (purity), Christian sex education is properly related to Gospel proclamation. The church makes its appeal for genuine repentance, not merely for feelings of sorrow or regret over a misdeed.

"Blessed are the pure in heart" is Gospel proclamation. It is saying that God does not impose on helpless sinners the need to achieve purity by themselves. Rather He extends the invitation to undergo His loving cardiac surgery. In the process the sinner is assured that he is forgiven, that Christ is his righteousness, and that purity is, after all, a gift of God's grace.

5

Sex Education and the Church's Ministry

Not everyone agrees concerning the need for, or the place of, sex education in the church setting. This is understandable. Until recently there has been an almost complete absence of dialog, few opportunities for looking at facts, for sharing opinions, for arriving at points of view.

5

SEX EDUCATION AND THE CHURCH'S MINISTRY

There was a time when Cal Moore referred to in chapter one would not have found Pastor Williams' office a sanctuary for his burden and guilt.

After 10 years of ministry, Rev. Williams took advantage of an extended vacation—a gift from his parish—to take stock of his decade of service. The first stages of the inventory were gratifying. Church membership had increased, attendance at worship services had improved, the number of parish organizations had doubled, and the educational program and facilities had been expanded. Weren't these the marks of a successful ministry?

Pastor Williams wasn't sure. He probed on. Deeper penetration became painful as another set of statistics registered in his consciousness. Somehow these figures did not lend themselves to organization in neat columns. Indeed, they were not the sort publicized in the annual parish report.

The statistics Pastor Williams found so painful broke down as divorces, infidelity, husband-wife tensions, quickly planned marriages, quiet arrangements for those whose free love wasn't so free at all, children trying to adjust to the misdeeds of men and women, and men and women trying to adjust to their own misdeeds. The significance of these negative statistics grew as Pastor Williams pondered the heartbreak and grief wrapped up in them.

Needless to say, Pastor Williams resolved that the second decade of his ministry would be different.

Taking Stock

This is the place to begin. We need to take stock. What have we been doing, and what have we accomplished? We need to do some soul-searching. This is difficult. We must be honest. We must be willing to be exposed. We have to look for forthright answers to blunt and perhaps distasteful facts. We cannot maneuver into some neutral corner and utter pacifying phrases, nor can we retreat into safety shelters and repeat the often-used cliches. There is no neutral corner, and the safety shelters have been bombed out.

It is not necessarily so that families that pray together stay together. Children who attend Sunday school and church regularly are not measurably better than those who do not. If church families were all solid and Sunday school children superior, the answer to our concern would be simple. Our pat answers would still hold true. But under the circumstances we had better ask new questions and find new answers.

The truth is that the church is not influencing its members to the degree we would like to believe. The older adults among us find this hard to accept because we are only too ready to acknowledge the influence the church had on our young lives. Perhaps it is we who can provide some revealing clues. As we carefully examine our childhood we might ask: Was it our faithful attendance at worship services and instruction classes that gave us our "mold"? Was it the message the church proclaimed? Or was it that our homelife put meaning into the lessons the church had taught? Was it the absence of temptations that made it possible for us to live sexually acceptable lives? Or is it that our sex life did not become a matter of record?

To question the influences that most affected our lives is of secondary importance. Our main concern is to determine the influences that contribute significantly to building the character of our growing generation. It is easy, in defense of a church that appears to be losing its "hold," to advance pet theories and countercharges against Hollywood, the TV industry, and against the purveyors of smut on the printed page. Perhaps these countercharges and tirades are necessary, and yet there are those who indicate that the sex climate of the United States would change very little even if the presses stopped, TV sets were turned off, and Hollywood would close shop. Perhaps it is true that these suggested causes are merely symptoms of a more serious sickness.

Not All Bad

It's a bit painful to stand by and see the church the target of harsh assaults. Are there explanations and answers that are honest?

Charges that the church is ineffective are charges against the church's organization, activities, and program. They are not charges against God or against the effective working of the Gospel. This leaves room for diligent meditation. It is at this point that Pastor Williams' standard of evaluation was challenged. Had the organization and the varied programs and activities ceased to be conveyors of Gospel proclamation?

Two questions can be posed at this point. The first is whether the message of the church has been essentially a Gospel-bearing witness. Messages of the "self-help" variety have been addressed to the burdens of the organization man. In effect, burdened man has been told, "Chin up, old boy. Think tall and smile. God is on your side, and everything will be fine." To young people we have had this bit of inspiration: "You're a fine group. We know you have problems. Stay out of trouble, and drive safely. You may not think so, but your parents are really okay. You'll understand when you grow up." We have talked about burdens and problems *but have been too silent about the curse of sin.* We have not grappled with the issues of life and death.

The second question is whether we, in our invitation to live the good life, have tended to dissect the Christian man and woman, to compartmentalize and categorize the Christian life. Perhaps we have placed a premium on violations of the Sixth Commandment and in so doing have minimized the overall injunction not only of the second table, which demands all-embracing love of the neighbor — man, woman, child — but also of the first table, which requires love of God "above all things." Could it be that sex sins are but symptoms of a deeper, more vicious unrighteousness?

That widespread reform does not follow in the wake of the church's work is not an indication of failure, for reform is not the measuring stick of the church's work. Church people can do and should do only what the Lord of the church has given His church to do. Making good people is not the church's business. If this is what the church has been trying to do, then perhaps it must admit defeat. If the church is performing its mission, it can claim success even in numbers of transformed lives, if for no other reason than that the Lord has assured success. In other words, every church worker can be assured of success—in God's terms—if he or she understands the mission of the church and performs it.

The above might be considered a restricted perspective. The apostle Paul understood this perspective. No doubt the experts of our time might devise a measuring instrument by which Paul's work would have to be assessed a failure. The Christian church knows of the success of Paul's work. Not everyone in Paul's audience became a statistic in the success columns of his ministry. Paul knew with whom he was waging war. He understood the Kingdom parables of the Lord and knew what "odds" were against him. With this perspective, under God he was successful.

As we evaluate various attempts to measure the church's effectiveness, we need to guard against those who would by cagey and clever ways discredit the church. We cannot be naive, but we must be honest.

A Claiming Ministry

Recently, while riding a train from Chicago to St. Louis, I began conversation with a gracious travel companion, a dentist from Minnesota. We identified ourselves and our occupations. This set the stage for conversation about the church. "I'll never forget the minister and the teacher I had when I was a kid. Church leaders are different today," was his first comment.

I was curious. "What do you mean?"

"There wasn't a sermon my minister preached that I didn't know he was talking to me and letting me know that the Lord wanted me. There wasn't a lesson in church school that didn't encourage me to look at my relationship with God.

"Once when I was in high school, Lud Schmidt, the youth leader, phoned and asked if I had time to go for a ride with him. He had noticed that I was hanging around with a pretty rough gang at school. He hadn't said anything to my folks about it, but he thought we should talk it over.

"A few days before I left for dental school the pastor talked to me. He came right to the point. He wanted me to come out of college a good dentist and a good Christian."

I assured him that he had been fortunate.

He continued: "Often when I was hearing a sermon or learning a lesson, I felt as if I were in a room with two doors. One was the Lord's, and the other was not. I was always being encouraged to open the Lord's door. The way it seems to me, nowadays the church acts as though there might be a third door—a kind of escape hatch. I just hope that my church still has men and women who can claim my son for the Lord the way I was."

In our scrutiny we need to ask a few questions about the claiming quality of our ministry. This involves an entirely new routine of ministering activity. It surrounds the pulpit and the classroom with a living hue; it leads footsteps to challenging addresses and invites conversations about troublesome but important issues. It is always claiming, claiming, claiming for the Lord. Sex education is part of this kind of ministry.

Am I Ready?

Most of us will agree that we received little or no sex education. What we learned was often from unreliable sources and out of personal curiosity. We learned the hard way—and often the wrong way. There were many things we should have learned but didn't; many things, perhaps, we should not have learned. It was difficult to think of sex as being good, a creation of God, for God-intended purposes, and for the good of wholesome men and women. We, too, learned the popular language of sex, and even today the words of proper sex language sound strange to us, and we don't know their meaning with certainty. This makes it difficult for us to converse.

We know the need for conversation, but we're not certain of what to say and how to say it. All of us find ourselves developing new attitudes and outlooks, but we don't feel at home with them. We don't know how to talk about sex.

The ancient proverb suggests that those who are to counsel and help others must first counsel and help themselves. It has been suggested that professional people of the church have a tendency to hide or to deny their own sexuality and by so doing attempt to create the impression that they have "risen above" the problem. This has dangerous implications. Sex is not a problem; it is a gift. This suggests a need for self-examination. We need to examine our own sex lives and attitudes. If we find distortions, we need to identify them, trace their sources, their outcomes. What happened to me as a result of them? Can we give distortion a new bend and a new shape? Can we fit ourselves and our way of life into the new mold? Time is required for the mold to harden.

We may even have to be so bold as to ask ourselves the question a psychology professor asked his students at the beginning of each semester: How normal are you? After allowing time for answering, he posed a second probing question. By what standard did you judge yourself? We take for granted that a self-analysis will be made in terms of the claiming ministry, whatever our church role might be.

A Look at Our Co-Workers

Not everyone agrees concerning the need for, or the place of, sex education in the church setting. This is understandable. Until recently there had been an almost complete absence of dialog, few opportunities for looking at facts, for sharing opinions, for arriving at points of view.

Perhaps there is truth in the statement of a Christian school teacher. "I feel that because I am concerned that children receive sex instruction, I am branded by my associates. They seem to think that this concern is a bit beneath their dignity." A pastor who is known to be an effective parish counselor vigorously maintains that his field is theology and that he has no time to be concerned with teaching sex facts to his members. Many of these critics need to be drawn into the conversation of these pages. Others feel inadequate because of personal experiences or lack of knowledge and instructional skills. Others are critical because they envision sex education as nothing more than reproduction instruction. (Were their assumptions correct, they would be justified in their criticism.)

Some years ago I received from a young seminarian a carbon copy of a class assignment entitled "A Parish Program of Sex Education." It was a series of graded courses on the "facts of life," based on the false assumption that a biological understanding of the human body is sufficient for developing a proper appreciation of sex and adequate skills in managing personal sexuality. I recall with considerable distaste the chapter "Sex Facts and the Christmas Story."

We need to be clear, for ourselves and for those whom we enlist to share our concern, as to what we mean by sex education. It is not a brash, blunt dispensing of heretofore classified information. It is not something to be advertised in bright red letters on the church bulletin boards. With dignity and accuracy and in proper language the children will learn essential facts, appreciations, and skills to help them not only understand and care for themselves but also understand and respect other people, be they male or female, brother or sister, father or mother. What they are taught will be fitted to the needs of their age. They will know they are wonderfully made by a God who gave father and mother the power to reproduce life. At the right time they will come to know and understand how this happens.

Fathers and mothers will be invited to join in the learning process and in the nurturing of their children.

Accomplishing this kind of program requires a teaching team—home, school, and church—that understands a program of sex education.

A Look at the Parish

In a summary way we can characterize the parish home as evidencing a general indifference to efforts directed to improving the moral standards and climate of a given community; often frustration arises from not knowing what to do. To a large degree these homes have turned over the responsibility of education to agencies outside the home. The school and its related agencies, the church and its organizational community, and a host of other community agencies and enterprises have invited the home to turn over its children to them. No doubt there is truth to the argument that these invitations were extended because in many instances homes were unwilling or unable to perform these functions acceptably. Homes have been willing or compelled, in various ways, to accept these invitations and have to a large extent relinquished their child-training privileges and responsibilities. This has freed the home to concentrate on the increasingly complicated business of making a living on an ever-rising standard. It has permitted the adult members of the family to become more and more involved in an organization-oriented society within the church and civic community. Finding transportation to get every member of the family to his or her appointed organizational activity has become a paramount family concern.

It would seem that the home is not altogether happy with the present arrangement, partly because members of the family are being drawn out of the home too frequently, and to a large extent because the home is not satisfied with the product of the agency-oriented training. The home feels victimized but finds it difficult to change existing patterns, and the children within the family insist on doing what everybody's children are doing.

The question is often raised whether sex education is the responsibility of the home or of the church. In reply, we would submit that because sex education concerns itself with teaching that sex is a gift of God and that the Christian's sex life is to be lived according to God's intended purposes and blessings, the church must be involved in sex education. Because the nurturing aspect of sex education can best be accomplished, as God intended, in the domestic setting, the Christian home is involved. The church and the home share responsibility.

On the basis of this statement the church's role becomes more obvious. The church must be concerned with teaching two generations at one time. It must teach children of all school-age levels the appropriate sex knowledge, attitudes, and skills. At the same time it must teach fathers and mothers the knowledge, attitudes, and skills required by their roles as males and females and as fathers and mothers of males and females. While doing this, the church must provide for parents the information and the nurturing skills necessary for them to assist their children in growing successfully as Christian boys and girls.

The cooperation of the home needs to be solicited in three ways. First, the home should support the church as it teaches children. Second, the home is to be involved in a learning-teaching role. Finally, in fulfilling its task the home must be open to the assistance of the church. Resistance can be expected as the home is drawn from its spirit of indifference into a participating relationship as a nurturing center. This has implications beyond the concern for sex education. In a sense this invitation is an invitation to the home to reclaim its right to be the training institution of the first order.

Perhaps the following note from a mother of a 9-year-old daughter and a teacher of young children is appropriate.

She writes: "I had the privilege of trying out some sex education material on my daughter before I presented it to my class. As we sat in the big chair, sharing the wonders of this great gift God has given us, I thought, 'How can I deprive the parents of the children in my class of this joy?' The closeness of a mother or father with one child, the repartee possible on a one-to-one basis, just cannot be duplicated in a classroom situation. Once a parent has tasted this closeness, he might well feel a teacher is usurping a great privilege from him if sex education is taken over by the school."

In comparatively few homes do the parents now provide their children with positive sex instruction and guidance. Some parents do not agree that such instruction is their responsibility. Others acknowledge the responsibility but plead inadequacy as the reason for not discussing sex with their children. A number of parents, with varying degrees of enthusiasm, would be happy to have the church provide sex instruction and guidance.

To meet such mixed attitudes and practices, any teaching and training program on sex should be well planned and then introduced with the least amount of fanfare, which might confirm indifference or, what is worse, arouse resistance.

Language Barriers

In emphasizing that sex education is more than reproduction education, there has been no intent to minimize the need for a thorough knowledge of sex facts. Genes—chromosomes—hormones. These are the words that help the pastor and the teacher develop insights and appreciation as pupils learn to confess, "I believe that God has made me." What a wonderful way to say that God is wise; that He has all power. What wonderful proof to support David's claim, "I am fearfully and wonderfully made."

If children are to learn to respect their bodies and body functions and organs, they will need to know respectable and dignified words to use as they speak and ask questions. For the teacher this will require study that gives accurate information and apt and precise words to relate that information.

An interesting problem arises at this point. Parents have repeatedly indicated that even after they have learned a new vocabulary, they find it difficult to use new terms and expressions. This is true of teachers also. The advice has been suggested that this can be overcome by repeatedly using these terms aloud and in private. Reading sex education books aloud, to self and to others, will help teachers and parents verbalize words they hesitate to speak to each other. Gradually a person comes to feel more comfortable and less shy. The added assurance is given that children and teen-agers lose their shyness quickly if the teacher displays an "at homeness" in this kind of conversation.

An unlearning process has to take place. As the teacher, the pastor, the parent introduces new terms, care will have to be taken to use explanatory phrases and illustrations so that new words are correctly understood. The phrases and illustrations will have to be carefully selected and practiced.

Children, teen-agers, and parents too, have often developed their own private language of sex. This language varies from home to home and from community to community. Occasionally this language is considered "cute." Some, as we know, is distasteful and filthy. The "cute" word can often be used as one describes and encourages the use of proper words. Most often children and parents are proud of possessing the knowledge and ability to use this new language. A 12-year-old girl confided to her mother that she was afraid to visit the doctor because she didn't know how to tell him about her personal problem. She didn't know the words to use.

I Wonder, I Wonder, a book for parents to read to primary children, helps families to use and know the meaning of a proper sex vocabulary. Here is Mrs. Frey's explanation of the meaning of uterus.

> "Inside every mother is a special baby-growing place. It has different names like womb or uterus. You're old enough now to call it by the grown-up name of uterus," said Daddy.
>
> "You-ter-us," said Julia, slowly. "It's not hard to say."
>
> "What does it look like? A crib?" John asked.
>
> "The uterus is shaped like a balloon with a little air blown into it." Daddy scratched a picture of it on the ground with a twig. "The walls are thicker though and are made of muscle. The walls stretch and the uterus gets big when a baby is growing in it. When the baby leaves, the walls shrink down again."
>
> "Where does the baby get out of the uterus?" asked John.
>
> "The uterus has an opening that looks pretty much like the opening at the bottom of a balloon. The baby leaves through this opening when it's all finished growing."

Each volume in the Concordia Sex Education Series aids in building a sex vocabulary suitable for the intended age group.

6

A Parish Program of Christian Sex Education

In describing a Christian program of sex education for Trinity Congregation, we have tried to (1) illustrate why it takes time and careful planning to initiate a worthwhile, ongoing program of sex education; (2) stress the need for integrating sex education with the overall parish program of Christian education; (3) show the need for involving parents in sex education within the parish educational program; (4) describe one organizational structure in which a program of sex education can be carried out; and (5) identify significant books and materials that will prove helpful in planning a Christian program of sex education.

6

A PARISH PROGRAM OF CHRISTIAN SEX EDUCATION

I am now ready to suggest ways in which a parish can conduct a Christian program of sex education. So far I have discussed the need for such instruction and, at least to some extent, the manner in which this can be carried out. It is time to be more specific. Here is an example of a Christian program of sex education in a fictitious congregation known as Trinity. The basic structure, procedure, and materials are those necessary in any parish program of Christian sex education.

The program is one that can be adapted or adopted by many congregations. Congregations that differ in size and structure from Trinity will find additional suggestions at the close of the chapter.

TRINITY PARISH DESCRIBED

Trinity Congregation, established in 1899, has a total membership of 852. Its pastor, F. Brown, is the only professional staff member. He is assisted by 28 lay teachers, some of whom are public school teachers. Trinity is located in Centerville, a city with a population of 15,000. Most members of the parish live in the city, a few in the neighboring rural community.

The Sunday school is the major agency for Christian instruction. The pastor conducts an instruction class for young people each Saturday morning during the school year. A Christian education building, now 3 years old, provides simple but adequate accommodations for the Sunday school. The Sunday school has enrolled 313 pupils of elementary school age, 43 of high school age, and 87 adults—age 21 and over. Pastor Brown, who has served the parish for 2 years, has given significant leadership in Christian education.

A Program of Christian Sex Education — How It Began

About a year after Pastor Brown's arrival in Centerville, the local newspaper published a series of articles exposing and denouncing the moral standards of the local teen-agers. Under the leadership of the local PTA, a "let's do something about it" campaign was started. As a result of this leadership the local ministerial association became involved. Pastor Brown was asked to serve as a committee of one to recommend one or more books that should be read, reviewed, and discussed by the association. During the following months these books were reviewed and discussed:

Bailey, Sherwin. *Sexual Ethics: A Christian View.* New York: The Macmillan Co., 1963.

Cole, William G. *Sex and Love in the Bible.* New York: Association Press, 1959.

Sex and the Church: A Sociological, Historical, and Theological Investigation of Sex Attitudes, ed. Oscar E. Feucht et al. St. Louis: Concordia Publishing House, 1961.

By September of that year, Pastor Brown was convinced that he had an assignment more significant than providing a bibliography on sex education for the ministerial association. Even though the public school officials had agreed to incorporate a moderate program of sex education in the school curriculum, Pastor Brown was not satisfied. Somehow he knew that sex education was the church's business. Would Trinity be receptive to such a program? Could an adequate program be developed for Trinity Parish? Where to begin? Pastor Brown knew it would take time. It would take careful planning.

Laying the Groundwork

Pastor Brown, we repeat, knew that initiating a program of Christian sex education in Trinity Church would take time and careful planning. The reader will profit by observing the step-by-step planning and procedure of Pastor Brown as he went about creating readiness in his congregation. In practice the steps were, of course, not as clean-cut as listed below. They were more interrelated and in some instances continued during the months of planning.

Step 1. *A Slow Start*

Pastor Brown was fully aware that it would be foolhardy to start too soon or too quickly. His ministry in and to the parish would have to continue as before. He did not want to become a fanatic on sex education, and he took care not to give the impression of being one. At first he arranged private conversations with members whose judgment he valued. The chairman of the parish board of education, several of the public school teachers, a businessman who had been on the local PTA committee, and a doctor were among the people whom he gradually involved. Briefly and simply Pastor Brown told his story and stated his concern. He invited those with whom he spoke to share his concern and to think and plan with him. During the following months the criticisms and suggestions of these people gave Pastor Brown encouragement and direction for further planning.

Step 2. *Drop a Hint*

While visiting parish homes and attending meetings of parish organizations, the pastor dropped hints of his concern. Now and then he made rather inconspicuous inquiries for the sake of eliciting reaction. He discovered that members of the congregation were concerned, at least to some extent, about the community moral climate. Many felt there was little they could do about it.

Step 3. *The Library Grows*

Without any particular fanfare, several volumes were added to the church library:

Narramore, Clyde M. *How to Tell Your Children About Sex.* Public Affairs Pamphlet No. 149. New York: The Public Affairs Committee, 1949. For parents.

Wolcott, Carolyn Muller. *God Made Me to Grow.* New York: Abingdon Press, 1960. For younger children.

Hulme, William A. *God, Sex, and Youth.* Englewood Cliffs, N. J.: Prentice-Hall, Inc., 1959. For adolescents.

Fields, Wilbert J. *Unity in Marriage.* St. Louis: Concordia Publishing House, 1962. For the engaged and married.

Step 4. *No Resolutions Yet*

Pastor Brown was anxious. He wanted to get something started. Was this the time to offer a proposal to the board of education? He talked it over with the chairman. On the agenda for the next meeting appeared an item something like this: "Is Trinity responsible for sex education?" The chairman decided to allow only 15 minutes for discussion of the question. One member reacted jokingly, asking what next. Another member wanted to start right away. "Let's launch a 6-week crash program." Mr. Stoddard, who was later to play an important role in the Trinity program, suggested, "I think the public schools can handle this better than we." The chairman then closed the discussion. No action was taken. Nothing was resolved, but the discussion had been begun. Pastor Brown was satisfied. At the close of the meeting he suggested that the members circulate his copy of *A Christian View of Sex Education.*

Step 5. *A Gentle Reminder*

In early fall Trinity was to observe a special Christian Family Week. Pastor Brown was preparing materials. His editorial for the *Trinity Beacon* reminded parishioners of the scandal that had been exposed by the local newspapers. The *Beacon* encouraged parents to become increasingly concerned and responsible in training, teaching, and nurturing the members of their family. With the regular mailing of the parish paper he included for each home a copy of a tract by Harry G. Coiner, "The Christian View of Sex" (St. Louis: Concordia Tract Mission, 1960).

Step 6. *Board Action*

It was time for the parish board of education to meet again. Mr. Stoddard suggested that the chairman place on the agenda the matter of Trinity's responsibility for Christian education on sex. "I think I've changed my mind," he said. "After reading *A Christian View of Sex Education,* I think we need to talk about the matter some more." At the board meeting it was decided to appoint a special committee, representative of the various age groups, for further study and consideration of Trinity Congregation's responsibility for providing a Christian program of sex instruction.

Step 7. *Special Committee Appointed*

The special committee was soon appointed, and its first meeting was called. Mr. Stoddard was elected chairman. All that the committee was able to accomplish the first night—it was a significant accomplishment—was that the members recognized that to serve effectively they would have to read and become better informed. They asked the parish board of education to provide them with adequate literature. Pastor Brown circulated the books that were already available, and Mr. Stoddard arranged with the chairman of the board of education to order additional materials. The following books were ordered:

Bracher, Marjory. *Love, Sex, and Life.* Philadelphia: Lutheran Church Press, 1964.

Hulme, William E. *Youth Considers Sex.* New York: Thomas Nelson & Sons, 1965.

Kirkendall, Lester A. *Understanding Sex.* Chicago: Science Research Associates, 1957.

Strain, Frances Bruce. *New Patterns in Sex Training,* rev. ed. New York: Appleton-Century-Crofts, Inc., 1951.

Thielicke, Helmut. *The Ethics of Sex,* trans. John W. Doberstein. New York: Harper & Row, 1964.

Step 8. *An Editorial*

Growing interest in the discussion became evident among the members of the parish. Some opposition was vocal. Pastor Brown was concerned. In preparing copy for the next issue of the *Trinity Beacon* he commented on the mixed reaction of the members. He stated that he was sympathetic with the various views expressed. He suggested that a clear definition of Christian sex education might be helpful. The definition he offered was both brief and simple. Christian sex education is a series of guided learning experiences to help a person grow in pertinent knowledge and understanding and to develop a wholesome attitude toward the role of sex in his private and social life, plus the willingness and ability to translate this knowledge, understanding, and attitude into conduct that will bring glory to God and benefit to himself and others. Such learning experiences are to enable the Christian to see clearly not only what he wants to do and be but also what he wants to avoid.

Furthermore, the editorial suggested that, properly understood, personal sex life is not to be separated from the full Christian life. The editorial was not argumentative but forthright and invited all members to share this parish concern.

Step 9. *Two Proposals*

At the second meeting of the special committee it was quite evident that the members had been reading. For one thing, they were more at ease as they exchanged insights, questioned one another, and weighed the matter of sex education with informed concern. Out of the meeting came two proposals to the parish board of education.

1. That this year's Christmas gift to each Sunday school teacher be a copy of *A Christian View of Sex Education* and that this book be the basis for a series of discussions under the guidance of the pastor.

2. That each member of the special committee be authorized to discuss with his respective group the issue of sex education, raising not the question, "Should Trinity Congregation provide a program of sex education?" but the more basic question, "Is there a need for a Christian program of sex education?" Affirmative reply to the latter question leads to another question, "Who, then, should provide such a program of sex education?"

The parish board of education concurred in both proposals of the special committee.

Step 10. *Christmastime*

Come Christmastime, the pastor's editorial in the *Trinity Beacon* pointed to the central concern of the season: "Let each of us put aside programing, planning, and projects. Let each of us focus attention on worshiping the Christ who is our Savior—the Christ who each day focuses His love and forgiveness on each of us."

Step 11. *A Difference of Opinion*

In January the Sunday school staff studied and evaluated the Christmas book along with other readings suggested by Pastor Brown. During the same month the members of the special committee began to share their questions and concerns with their respective organizations and age groups. By February things were beginning to happen. The pastor was delighted to note the enthusiasm of many of the Sunday school teachers and to learn the new insights and understandings the members of the staff reported. One teacher commented, "Now I see my pupils in a new light and understand the purpose of my teaching in a new way." The special committee recommended to the board of education that a special curriculum committee be appointed to evaluate and then propose a Christian program of sex education for the congregation.

In the opinion of the committee no further recommendation could be made before review of such a proposal. The recommendation to the parish board of education took into consideration the members' responses, which revealed general agreement that there was need for Christian sex education but divided opinion whether such education was properly the responsibility only of the home or also of the church.

Step 12. *Curriculum Committee*

The proposed curriculum committee on sex education was appointed. The five members were two teachers from the public school; a doctor; a mother; also a nurse; Mr. Stoddard, as liaison between the committee and the board of education; and Mrs. Elva Trumbull, who for years had borne responsibility for the church library.

Step 13. *Ready to Go*

By late spring the curriculum committee was ready with several proposals. These were reviewed by the original committee, the board of education, and the Sunday school staff. A single program was agreed on. It was further agreed to begin the program with the new school year in September. It was suggested, however, that before launching the program of sex education the board of education review the whole parish educational program. According to the curriculum committee, the program of sex education should be incorporated in the overall parish program of Christian education.

The Essentials of Christian Education

The curriculum committee had done its work well. With it the parish board of education agreed that for effectiveness the proposed program of sex education should not be developed separately. From the very start, sex education should be carefully planned as an integral part of the ongoing parish program of Christian education.

To prepare the way for such planning, the committee took the bold step of recommending that the whole parish program of Christian instruction be reevaluated. For the sake of more careful analysis, the committee suggested that the reevaluation proceed by raising three crucial questions.

How Big Is Our Concept of Christian Education?

Through review of its concept of Christian education the board of education concluded that Christian education is more than an agency activity, a program thrust, or a phase of church work. Christian education is a process of—

1. Proclaiming the good news that God cares.
2. Nurturing God's children.
3. Helping God's children grow to "the stature of the fullness of Christ."
4. Helping God's children grow in grace and knowledge.
5. Equipping God's children for every good work.
6. Teaching God's children to minister to one another.
7. Leading God's children into a life of discipleship.

The life of a congregation depends on this kind of education. Such education involves every member of the parish, for even the adults remain God's children who are to continue to grow up into Christ.

Sex education, the board concluded, is properly part of this essential Christian preparation for assuming an adult role in church and society.

What Is the Role of God's Word in Christian Education?

Pastor Brown helped the board answer the second question. He suggested that God's Word is a kind of power tool. In support he pointed out that God's Word—

1. Is a powerful word (Heb. 4:12).
2. Is a power unto salvation (Rom. 1:16).
3. Possesses life and spirit (John 6:63).
4. Regenerates (1 Peter 1:23).
5. Works repentance and converts (2 Tim. 2:25).
6. Purifies (John 15:3).
7. Bestows faith (John 1:7).
8. Saves (James 1:21).
9. Gives life (2 Cor. 3:6).
10. Makes holy (2 Tim. 4:5).

"Let's not forget," reminded Pastor Brown, "the Spirit of God is at work in the Word." From the explanation of the Third Article he added that the Holy Spirit "*calls, gathers, enlightens,* and *sanctifies* the whole Christian church on earth and *keeps* it with Jesus Christ in the one true faith."

God's Word, the board concluded, is the active agent in Christian education. People, young and old, who are not in the Word will find it difficult to be filled with the Spirit and to live their lives "in Christ." Any program of Christian education, including any program of Christian sex education, has to grow out of the working Word and the activity of the Holy Spirit.

How Are Parents Involved in Christian Education?

How quickly the implications of this third question became apparent to the parish board of education! After all, the board members had often expressed concern about the passive attitude of many fathers and mothers in the parish.

Again the members of the board found themselves in agreement. The home is to be the basic agency in Christian nurture. The Word of the Lord is to be in the hearts of fathers and mothers. They are to talk and teach this Word to their children all day long (Deut. 6:4-9). This heart-to-heart talking takes place best in the context of the home. There is no alternative to strengthening the homes of the parish as nurturing centers. In them God's children of all ages are to grow as together they become more fully people in Christ.

Here again the conclusion seemed obvious. A successful program of religious instruction or Christian sex education is dependent on the nurturing activity of the home.

A Readiness Program

The September emphasis for Trinity was "Christian Education." For Pastor Brown and the board of education it was an opportunity to acquaint the entire membership with their concerns and activities during the past year. During September the sermons elaborated on the three evaluation questions discussed previously by the board. According to custom, two special family nights were planned. The *Trinity Beacon* and additional publicity announced that these family-night meetings were to be very special. As a result, attendance was above average each night. Step by step the members of the board carefully presented their proposals for a revitalized program of Christian education for Trinity Congregation. They spoke of need, program and organization, and of desired outcomes and goals.

According to the board proposal, all parents with children enrolled in the Sunday school were invited to attend parent instruction-discussion classes. Parents would be divided into three groups: primary, intermediate, and high school. Each group was to meet once a month on Sunday morning during the Sunday school hour. Primary department parents would meet on the first Sunday of each month, intermediate department parents the second Sunday, high school department parents the third Sunday.

"What are we going to study?" asked one parent.

Pastor Brown smiled a bit. He was hoping someone would ask this question. "Each Sunday," the pastor began to answer, "your children study, from leaflets or booklets, lessons and stories from Scripture. We are proposing," the pastor continued, "that fathers and mothers study in the Bible the same lessons that the children are learning from their leaflets and booklets. These lessons are not only for little children; they are also for God's big children.

"We intend to divide each session into two parts. During the first half-hour we will seek to understand the meaning of the lesson for our lives. During the second half-hour we will discuss ways in which parents can help children know and live the truth of the lessons they have learned."

Some parents smiled as they saw themselves sitting in Sunday school again. Most of them realized it would take some doing to get into the habit of attending regularly, but somehow the proposal made sense to them. They seemed willing to give it a try.

"From time to time," Pastor Brown explained, "for variety's sake we will study and discuss topics of special interest." He pointed to a display table at the rear of the room. On it were copies of several parent guidance booklets. He mentioned also a display of sex education booklets and materials that he had selected from the library. "These are some of the materials we hope to use in both parents' and children's classes. In addition, we intend to use many fine films and filmstrips that are available to us."

Trinity's Story Summarized

Because Trinity Parish is a simulated parish, we must discontinue our narrative at this point. We would like to continue; we would like to make this narrative a success story. We believe that it could be.

In describing a Christian program of sex education for Trinity Congregation, we have tried to (1) illustrate why it takes time and careful planning to initiate a worthwhile, ongoing program of sex education; (2) stress the need for integrating sex education with the overall parish program of Christian education; (3) show the need for involving parents in sex education within the parish educational program; (4) describe one organizational structure in which a program of sex education can be carried out; and (5) identify significant books and materials that will prove helpful in planning a Christian program of sex education.

To complete the story of Trinity, we might add the following. After the parent classes had met several times, the parish board of education and Pastor Brown felt that it was time to introduce a formal program of Christian sex education.

The board agreed on the following program.

A Program of Christian Sex Education

Staff: Pastor Brown

Mrs. Norman Stennett — Member of Trinity Sunday School staff and public school nurse.

Dr. Warren Simon — Member of the Trinity Bible Class staff

Sunday School Staff

The Sunday school staff assisted in preparing the Christian sex education program. For several months the teachers prepared themselves for service as teachers in the Christian sex education program. Under the direction of the pastor, Dr. Simon, and Mrs. Stennett, these teachers will utilize the various materials listed below. These materials are to be used as appropriate according to the regular Sunday lesson emphasis. In all instances the parents are to have opportunity to become acquainted with the materials before presentation to the children.

MATERIALS AND AGE GROUP

Age Group	*Materials*
Kindergarten Through Grade 3	*I Wonder, I Wonder,* by Marguerite Kurth Frey
Parents of Kindergarten to Grade 3	*Parents Guide to Christian Conversation About Sex,* by Erwin J. Kolb
	Parents' Responsibility, by Marion O. Lerrigo and Helen Southard
Intermediate Grades	*Wonderfully Made,* by Ruth Stevenson Hummel
	A Story About You, by Marion O. Lerrigo and Helen Southard
Parents of Intermediate Grades	*Parents Guide to Christian Conversation About Sex,* by Erwin J. Kolb
	How to Tell Your Children About Sex, by Clyde M. Narramor
Junior High School Pupils	*Take the High Road,* by August J. Bueltmann

	Finding Yourself, by Marion O. Lerrigo and Helen Southard
Parents of Junior High School Pupils	*Parents Guide to Christian Conversation About Sex,* by Erwin J. Kolb
High School Students	*Life Can Be Sexual,* by Elmer N. Witt,
	Sorting Things Out, by U. C. Warner
For Parents of High Schoolers	*Parents Guide to Christian Conversation About Sex,* by Erwin J. Kolb
	Preparing Your Children for Marriage, by W. Clark Ellzey
Engaged Couples	*Unity in Marriage,* by W. J. Fields
	Building a Christian Marriage, by William E. Hulme
	Marriage Counseling Cards
Married Couples	*Facing Problems of Modern Marriage* (Kit)
	Being Married, by Evelyn M. Duvall and Reuben Hill

ORGANIZATION OF CLASSES

Sunday School Pupils (K through Grade 8)	The Sunday school staff, with the assistance of Dr. Simon and Mrs. Stennett, will utilize the materials listed above at appropriate times during regular Sunday school sessions.
Parents (K through Grade 3)	Will meet the first Sunday of each month during regular Sunday school hour. Staff: Pastor Brown and others.
Parents Intermediate grades	Will meet the second Sunday of each month during regular Sunday school hour. Staff: Pastor Brown and others.
Parents Junior and Senior High School	Will meet the third Sunday of each month during regular Sunday school hour. Staff: Pastor Brown and others.
High School Students Grades 8, 9, and 10	Pastor's instruction classes Wednesday afternoons and Saturday mornings. Staff: Pastor Brown.
High School Students Grades 11 and 12	Will meet the fourth Sunday of each month during regular Sunday school hour. Staff: Pastor Brown and others.
Engaged Couples	Engaged couples should announce their intent of marriage sufficiently early to allow for a minimum of four coun-

	seling sessions prior to their wedding date. Counseling sessions following marriage are encouraged. Tuesday nights from 7 to 8 or from 9:30 to 10:30 are set aside for this purpose. Staff: Pastor Brown and Dr. Simon.
Married Couples	Pastor Brown available anytime by appointment.

Program and Organization Options

Congregations vary in size, geographic location, program structure, physical facilities, size and ability of staff. Each congregation has its own personality, its own needs, and its own goals and objectives. Much of what has been said about the Trinity Congregation program of Christian sex education can apply to a large number of congregations in spite of the differences among them. The following comments and suggestions may be helpful to congregations whose structure and size and organization vary from that of the congregation just described.

The Parish with a Christian Elementary School

The congregation that maintains a Christian elementary school possesses enviable resources for initiating and maintaining a program of Christian sex instruction. We can assume it has the resources of staff, facilities, organization, and rather free entrance into the homes of the parish.

Start with the school staff. Here is a significant potential that needs to be developed. Many of the concerns and understandings discussed in earlier chapters of this volume will have to be grasped and shared by members of a school staff. We cannot assume that teachers possess the adequate knowledge, understanding, and "at homeness" needed in applying sex knowledge and understandings to themselves or to their pupils. As this "at homeness" develops, time will have to be allowed for the study of curricular materials on appropriate grade levels. Again we stress that Christian sex education should not be an isolated activity, but an integrated part of a program of Christian instruction.

Several suggestions are in order. First, staff members should study *A Christian View of Sex Education* along with the other volumes of this sex education series. The bibliography in this volume lists additional books and periodicals. Second, a study of the school's curriculum guide will help determine the significant opportunities, both formal and informal, for including sex instruction and guided learning experiences. (See *A Curriculum Guide for Lutheran Elementary Schools*, 3 vols. [St. Louis: Concordia Publishing House], and Helen Manley, *A Curriculum Guide in Sex Education* [St. Louis: State Publishing Co.].) Third, select texts and instructional material for classroom and library for pupils and for parents.

Even though the Christian elementary school provides maximum hours for instruction and nurture, these additional hours do not offset the need for parent involvement in Christian nurture. The Christian home provides the best setting for both situational and relational teaching. First of all the goodwill and support of the parents will have to be sought. Second, fathers and mothers will have to be equipped to carry out their nurturing role. In some Christian elementary schools the involvement of parents in Christian education has been reasonably well achieved. If not, here is the place to begin. Parents will have to be drawn in and equipped to carry out more fully their role as Christian fathers and mothers. A program of Christian sex instruction will be better received by parents and pupils and be assured of greater ongoing success if it thus becomes part of an overall program of Christian sex education.

I am acquainted with a parish where each professional member of the school staff meets once a month, September through April, with the parents of the children enrolled in his class. Here is a ready-made organizational structure into which a program of Christian sex education can be effectively introduced. In this connection one suggestion should be considered: few parishes with an elementary school are able to enroll every parish family in the school. In such instances teachers often focus their attention only on the children enrolled in school and their parents. Those children not enrolled and their parents should always be included as a chief concern of the school staff's ministry to its members.

Frequently members of a school staff serve the parish in capacities such as Sunday school director, youth counselor, or scout leader. It seems only natural that when such a staff member has become equipped to provide Christian sex instruction for the school program, he would also be anxious and ready to provide this specialized ministry to other groups or individuals assigned to his care.

Some churches maintain Christian secondary schools. The suggestions given for Christian elementary schools apply equally to high schools. High school principals and guidance counselors can do much to encourage the introduction and development of a program of Christian sex education with the Christian school. This will require not only an adequate program of instruction for students but also learning opportunities for staff members to gain new insights and adequate understandings concerning sex and Christian sex education.

A Parish with a Weekday School

More and more parishes are realizing that one Sunday school hour per week for Christian instruction is not sufficient. For the congregation with a weekday school the suggestions and comments made concerning Trinity Parish and the parish with a Christian elementary school can, by adopting and adapting, serve the parish with the weekday school program. For the parish that feels its program of Christian education isn't adequate we commend the possibility of initiating a weekday program. Here is a potential not only for accomplishing a program of Christian sex instruction but also doubling and tripling the number of hours of the total parish Christian education program.

Small Parishes

The small white frame church with its shiny spire and cross is still a commonplace scene for many Americans. Many denominations have large numbers of members whose names are recorded on the roles of small parishes. Congregations with memberships of 200 to 300 people often feel their resources too limited to offer more than a minimum ministry. Often these parishes have to share their minister with one or more area congregations.

Minimum staff and membership resources may present a real problem and challenge. For a variety of reasons, smaller congregations often find it difficult to consolidate or affiliate with other congregations. Some of them are finding that by pooling both staff and membership resources, additional ministries and service can be provided. The great variety of ways in which such cooperation may be feasible makes it difficult to describe an ideal procedure.

The purpose for our calling attention to it here is merely to suggest that a number of parishes may join forces and resources and thus be able to provide a reasonably comprehensive program, not only of Christian education but of Christian sex instruction. The above suggestion in no way is intended to leave the impression that a small parish cannot, by itself, have the essentials of Christian sex instruction.

A Final Word

Paul, 4 years of age, was anxiously awaiting his visit to Grandmother's house. He was looking forward to showing Grandmother what a big boy he was. He could brush his teeth and wash his hands and face by himself. He didn't need anyone to help him.

What a disappointment when Paul came to Grandmother's house! There he found he was not able to impress Grandmother with all the things he had learned to do for himself. Why? At Grandmother's sink was no footstool such as he had at home. Grandmother sensed his need and soon purchased a little footstool for him.

On the footstool was some appropriate verse. It read like this:

> This little stool belongs to me.
> It makes me happy as can be.
> Now I can reach things that before I couldn't
> And many times the things I shouldn't.

As time went on, Paul found places other than the sink where the footstool was useful. Sometimes he was found reaching for things he "shouldn't." Grandmother was patient and helpful as she guided Paul in making proper use of his new tool.

Basic for boys and girls, teen-agers, and young adults is a solid foundation of sexual information on which to stand firm as they reach for maturity. But even more than this "footstool," they need the mature and patient guidance of loved ones, teachers and parents, who will inspire them to wholesome attitudes and aid them in reaching for full sexual maturity with discernment and good judgment.

A Resource List

For the Christian Sex Educator

BOOKS

For Parents

Amstutz, H. Clair. *Growing Up to Love: A Guide to Sex Education for Parents.* Scottdale, Pa.: Herald Press, 1956. 103 pp. $2.50.

Baruch, Dorothy Walter. *New Ways in Sex Education: A Guide for Parents and Teachers.* New York: McGraw-Hill Book Co., 1959. 256 pp. $4.95. Also available in a Bantam Books paperback, 60 cents.

Child Study Association of America. *What to Tell Your Children About Sex,* rev. ed. Des Moines, Iowa: Meredith Press, 1964. 117 pp. $2.95.

Coiner, Harry G. *The Christian View of Sex.* St. Louis: Concordia Tract Mission, 1960. 17 pp. 5 cents each, $5.00 per 100.

Driver, Helen I., ed. *Sex Guidance for Your Child: A Parent Handbook.* Madison, Wis.: Monona Publications, 1960. 192 pp. $4.50.

Eckert, Ralph G. *Sex Attitudes in the Home.* New York: Association Press, 1956. 242 pp. Paper, 35 cents; cloth, $3.50. Also available as a Popular Library paperback, 50 cents.

Ellzey, W. Clark. *Preparing Your Children for Marriage.* New York: Association Press, 1964. 159 pp. $3.95.

Hymes, James L., Jr. *How to Tell Your Child About Sex.* New York: Public Affairs Pamphlets, 1949. 28 pp. 25 cents.

Kolb, Erwin J. *Parents Guide to Christian Conversation About Sex.* St. Louis: Concordia Publishing House, 1967. 144 pp. $1.95.

Lorand, Rhoda L. *Love, Sex and the Teenager.* New York: The Macmillan Co., 1965. $4.95.

Narramore, Clyde M. *How to Tell Your Children About Sex.* Grand Rapids, Mich.: Zondervan Publishing House, 1958. 97 pp. Paper, $1.00; cloth, $1.95.

Pike, James A. *Teenagers and Sex*. Englewood Cliffs, N. J.: Prentice-Hall, Inc., 1965. 146 pp. $3.95.

For Younger Children

Appell, Clara, Morey Appell, and Suzanne Szasz. *We Are Six: The Story of a Family*. New York: Golden Press, 1959. 61 pp. $2.99.

De Schweinitz, Karl. *Growing Up: The Story of How We Became Alive, Are Born, and Grow Up*, 4th ed. New York: The Macmillan Co., 1965. 54 pp. $2.95.

Frey, Marguerite Kurth. *I Wonder, I Wonder*. St. Louis: Concordia Publishing House, 1967. 30 pp. $1.75. K—grade 3.

Gruenberg, Sidonie Matsner. *The Wonderful Story of How You Were Born*. Garden City, N. Y.: Doubleday & Co., 1952. 39 pp. $2.95.

Hummel, Ruth Stevenson. *Wonderfully Made*. St. Louis: Concordia Publishing House, 1967. 46 pp. $1.75. Grades 4—6.

Levine, Milton I., and Jean H. Seligmann. *A Baby Is Born*, rev. ed. New York: Golden Press, 1962. 53 pp. $1.95.

Whiting, Ellis W. *The Story of Life*. Milwaukee: Hammond Publishing Co., 1957. 48 pp. $1.00.

Wolcott, Carolyn Muller. *God Made Me To Grow*. New York: Abingdon Press, 1960. 24 pp. $1.50.

For Preadolescents

Bueltmann, August J. *Take the High Road*. St. Louis: Concordia Publishing House, 1967. 88 pp. $1.95. Grades 7—9.

Clarkson, E. Margaret. *Chats With Young People On Growing Up*. Grand Rapids, Mich.: Wm. B. Eerdmans Publishing Co., 1962. 93 pp. $2.50.

Levine, Milton I., and Jean H. Seligmann. *The Wonder of Life: How We Are Born and How We Grow Up*. New York: Golden Press, 1952. 116 pp. $2.95.

Scheinfeld, Amram. *Why You Are You*. New York: Abelard-Schuman, 1959. 171 pp. $3.50.

Strain, Frances Bruce. *Being Born*. New York: Appleton-Century-Crofts, Inc., 1954. 144 pp. $2.95.

For Adolescents

Adams, Clifford R. *Looking Ahead to Marriage*. Chicago: Science Research Associates, 1954. 48 pp. 60 cents.

Bauer, W. W. *Moving Into Manhood*. Garden City, N. Y.: Doubleday & Co., 1963. 107 pp. $2.95.

Beck, Lester F. *Human Growth*. New York: Harcourt, Brace & World, 1949. 128 pp. $3.50.

Behlmer, Reuben B. *From Teens to Marriage*. St. Louis: Concordia Publishing House, 1959. 112 pp. $1.95.

Dickerson, Roy E. *So Youth May Know: Sex Education for Youth.* New York: Association Press, 1948. 259 pp. $3.50.

Duvall, Evelyn Millis. *Love and the Facts of Life.* New York: Association Press, 1963. 352 pp. $4.95.

————. *Why Wait Till Marriage?* New York: Association Press, 1965. 128 pp. $2.95.

Hettlinger, Richard F. *Living With Sex: The Student's Dilemma.* New York: Seabury Press, 1966. 190 pp. $4.95.

Hulme, William E. *God, Sex, and Youth.* Englewood Cliffs, N. J.: Prentice-Hall, Inc., 1959. 179 pp. $3.95.

————. *Youth Considers Sex.* New York: Thomas Nelson & Sons, 1965. 95 pp. $1.50.

Johnson, Charlene. *Altogether Lovely: A Book for Teen-Age Girls.* Philadelphia: Fortress Press, 1960. 112 pp. $2.50.

Jones, G. Curtis. *Youth Deserves to Know.* New York: The Macmilllan Co., 1958. 134 pp. $3.95.

Kirkendall, Lester A. *Understanding Sex.* Chicago: Science Research Associates, 1957. 48 pp. 60 cents.

Osborne, Ernest G. *Understanding Your Parents.* New York: Association Press, 1962. 122 pp. 75 cents.

Riess, Walter *The Teen-Ager You're Dating: A Christian View of Sex.* St. Louis: Concordia Publishing House, 1964. 127 pp. $1.00.

Vetter, Marjorie, and Laura Vitray. *The Questions Girls Ask.* New York: E. P. Dutton & Co., 1959. 156 pp. $2.95.

Witt, Elmer. *Life Can Be Sexual.* St. Louis: Concordia Publishing House, 1967. Price to be announced.

For the Engaged and Married

Bainton, Roland H. *What Christianity Says About Sex, Love, and Marriage.* New York: Association Press, 1957. 124 pp. 75 cents.

Babbage, Stuart Barton. *Christianity and Sex.* Chicago: Inter-Varsity Press, 1963. 59 pp. $1.25.

Duvall, Evelyn M., and Reuben Hill. *Being Married.* New York: Association Press, 1960. 440 pp. $4.95.

Fields, Wilbert J. *Unity in Marriage.* St. Louis: Concordia Publishing House, 1962. 168 pp. $3.00.

Flanagan, Geraldine Lux. *The First Nine Months of Life.* New York: Simon and Schuster, Inc., 1962. 95 pp. $3.95.

Guttmacher, Alan F. *The Complete Book of Birth Control.* New York: Ballantine Books, 1963. 152 pp. 50 cents.

Hulme, William E. *Building a Christian Marriage.* Englewood Cliffs, N. J.: Prentice-Hall, Inc., 1965. $3.50.

Jonsson, G., and L. Jonsson. *Can Two Become One?* Philadelphia: Fortress Press, 1965. 121 pp. $1.25.

Popenoe, Paul. *Sex, Love, and Marriage.* New York: Belmont Books, 1963. 173 pp. 50 cents.

Rehwinkel, Alfred M. *Planned Parenthood and Birth Control in the Light of Christian Ethics.* St. Louis: Concordia Publishing House, 1959. 120 pp. Paper, $1.50; cloth, $2.25.

For Older Adults

Lewin, S. A., and John Gilmore. *Sex After Forty.* New York: Medical Research Press. $3.50.

Rubin, I. *Sexual Life After Sixty.* New York: Basic Books, 1965. 274 pp. $5.95.

Saxe, Louis P., and Noel B. Gerson. *Sex and the Mature Man.* New York: Julian Messher, Inc., 1964. $5.95.

For the Serious Student

Bailey, Derrick Sherwin. *Sexual Relation in Christian Thought.* New York: Harper & Row, 1959. 312 pp. $4.50

Bailey, Sherwin. *Sexual Ethics: A Christian View.* New York: The Macmillan Co., 1963. 159 pp. $1.45.

Colacci, Mario. *Christian Marriage Today: A Comparison of Roman Catholic and Protestant Views,* rev. ed. Minneapolis: Augsburg Publishing House, 1965. 203 pp. $1.95.

Demant, V. *Christian Sex Ethics.* New York: Harper & Row, 1965. $2.75.

Duvall, Evelyn M., and Sylvanus M. Duvall. *Sex Ways: In Fact and Faith.* New York: Association Press, 1961. 253 pp. $3.95.

Feucht, Oscar E., et al., eds. *Sex and the Church: A Sociological, Historical, and Theological Investigation of Sex Attitudes.* St. Louis: Concordia Publishing House, 1961. 277 pp. $3.50.

Piper, Otto A. *The Biblical View of Sex and Marriage.* New York: Charles Scribner's Sons, 1960. 239 pp. $3.95.

Rainer, Jerome, and Julia Rainer. *Sexual Adventure in Marriage.* New York: Julian Messner, Inc., 1964. 256 pp. $5.95.

Thielicke, Helmut. *The Ethics of Sex.* New York: Harper & Row, 1964. 338 pp. $4.95.

For the Program Planner

Batten, Charles E., and Donald E. McLean. *Fit To Be Tied: An Approach to Sex Education and Christian Marriage.* Greenwich, Conn.: Seabury Press, 1960. 124 pp. $1.95. (Outlines a 4-session course for church youth groups)

Bracher, Marjory. *Love, Sex, and Life.* Philadelphia: Lutheran Church Press, 1964. Pupil text, 152 pp., $1.25; Teacher's Guide, 57 pp. $1.25. (A 6- to 10-session course for 15- and 16-year-olds)

Kirkendall, Lester A. *Sex Education As Human Relations: A Guidebook on Content and Methods for School Authorities and Teachers.* New York: Inor Publishing Co., 1950. 351 pp. $4.50.

Wessler, Martin F. *Christian View of Sex Education.* St. Louis: Concordia Publishing House, 1967. 88 pp. $1.95.

Lampe, Viola, and Carl Gorham. *Growing Up: Social Health Education Guide, Grade Six,* rev. ed. San Diego, Calif.: San Diego City Schools, 1965. viii and 106 pp. (Outlines a 5-lesson sex education course)

Lerrigo, Marion O., et al. *Sex Education Series.* Chicago: American Medical Association, 1960—62. Titles: *Parents' Responsibility* (for parents of preschool and primary children); *Facts Aren't Enough* (for adults responsible for children); *A Story About You* (for children 9—12); *Finding Yourself* (for children 12—15); *Approaching Adulthood* (for ages 16—20). 30 cents each.

Manley, Helen. *A Curriculum Guide in Sex Education.* St. Louis: State Publishing Co., 1964. 59 pp. $1.25.

Southard, Helen F. *Sex Morality-Teaching Record Kit.* Two 33⅓ rpm records, three sets of program materials, one pamphlet. Records contain two talks by Mrs. Southard, a discussion by college students, and talks by a minister and a psychiatrist. Kit price, $10. Additional program materials, $1.00 per set; additional pamphlets, 75 cents each. Available from Bureau of Communications, National Board, YWCA, 600 Lexington Ave., New York, N. Y. 10022.

Warner, Hugh C. *Sex Education Booklets.* St. Louis: Concordia Publishing House. 1963. Titles: *Puzzled Parents: Where Did I Come From?* (for young children); *How a Family Begins* (for early adolescent girls); *The Start of a Family* (for early adolescent boys); *Science and You* (for later adolescents); *Sorting Things Out* (for later adolescents and young adults); *The Christian View of Sex* (for the serious student). 35 cents each, $2.00 per set.

Wier, Frank E. *Sex and the Whole Person.* New York: Abingdon Press, 1962. Pupil text, 48 pp., 60 cents; Leader's Guide, 64 pp., $1.00. (An 8-session course for teen-age Christians.)

FILMS, FILMSTRIPS, SLIDES, AND TAPES

For Younger Children

How Babies Are Made. Thirty-two 35 mm. color slides, 15 min., printed commentary. Creative Scope, Inc., 1965. Available from Creative Scope, Inc., 509 Fifth Ave., New York, N. Y. 10017. Slides, commentary, and viewer, $12.

I Wonder, I Wonder. Color filmstrip with recording (15 min.), 79-3100, $10.

Part of the Concordia Sex Education Series, this filmstrip and record are based on the book of the same title and are designed for ages 5—8.

A delightful presentation of basic and elementary information from a Christian viewpoint. A very natural handling of the subject within the framework of a family.

For Preadolescents

The Miracle of Reproduction. Film, 15 min., black-and-white or color. Sid Davis Productions, 1954. Available from university and other film libraries. Rental rates will vary.

Wonderfully Made. Color filmstrip with recording (15 min.), 79-3101, $10.

For use with ages 9—11, the filmstrip and recording are based on the Concordia Sex Education Series book of the same title. The sound filmstrip presents the wonders of body and mind and helps prepare this age level for physical and emotional change.

For Early Adolescents

The Human Body: Reproductive System. Film, 14 min., black-and-white or color. Coronet Films, 1959. Available from university and other film libraries. Rental rates will vary.

Human Growth, sec. ed. Film, 19 min., color. Wexler Films, for the E. C. Brown Trust, 1962. Available from university and other film libraries. Rental, $3.

Take the High Road. Color filmstrip with recording (15 min.), 79-3102, $10.

The third sound filmstrip in the Concordia Sex Education Series, based on the book of the same title. In addition to presenting and reviewing the wonders of the human body and reproduction, the sound filmstrip deals with the transition from adolescence to adulthood, proper attitudes, and fundamental factors in the relationships of girls and boys. For ages 12—14.

For Later Adolescents and Young Adults

A Basis for Sex Morality series. Six sound, color filmstrips: *Love, Friendship, and Marriage* (17 min.), *The Nature of Sex* (18 min.), *The Man-Woman Relationship* (18 min.), *Pre-Marital Relationships* (18 min.), *Rationalizing Sex Behavior* (14 min.), *Guidelines for Sex Behavior* (18 min.). Illustrated lectures by the Rev. Canon Brian Green to college students. Cathedral Films, 1964. Available from Audiovisual Aids Service, Concordia Publishing House, 3558 S. Jefferson Ave., St. Louis, Mo. 63118. With guide, $7 each; with 33⅓ rpm record and guide, $10 each; complete kit, $45.90.

Human Reproduction, rev. ed. Film, 21 min., black-and-white or color. McGraw-Hill Textfilms, 1965. Available from university and other film libraries. Rental rates will vary.

Marriage Counseling kit. Four sound, color filmstrips: *Marriage Makes a Difference* (40 frames, 7 min.), *Marriage Requires Adjustments* (46 frames, 8 min.), *The Intimacies of Marriage* (40 frames, 8 min.), and *Making Marriage Last* (40 frames, 8 min.). Family Films, 1960. Available from Audiovisual Aids Service, Concordia Publishing House, 3558 S. Jefferson Ave., St. Louis, Mo. 63118. With guide, $6.50 each; with 33⅓ rpm record and guide, $10 each; complete kit, $25.50.

The Moral Choice. Film, 30 min., black-and-white. Cathedral Films, 1965. Available from Audiovisual Aids Service, Concordia Publishing House, 3558 S. Jefferson Ave., St. Louis, Mo. 63118. Rental, $10.

NOTE: For additional listing see biennial *Audio-Visual Resource Guide* produced by Department of Audio-Visual and Broadcast Education, Division of Christian Education, National Council of the Churches of Christ in the U. S. A., 475 Riverside Dr., New York, N. Y. 10027.

For Parents

Parents Guide to Christian Conversation About Sex. Color filmstrip with recording (15 min.), 79-3103, $10.

An excellent production for use in parents' groups, Parent-Teacher League meetings, etc., to help Christian parents provide sound sex education for their children. Part of the Concordia Sex Education Series.

Counseling Aids

Glassberg, B. Y. *Teen-Age Sex Counselor*. Great Neck, N. Y.: Barron's Educational Series, 1965. 138 pp. $1.25.

Marriage Counseling Cards. A set of 44 cards to help counsel couples planning marriage. Prepared by the Family Life Committee of the Board of Parish Education of The Lutheran Church — Missouri Synod. St. Louis: Concordia Publishing House, 1962. $3.

Morris, J. Kenneth. *Marriage Counseling: A Manual for Ministers*. Englewood Cliffs, N. J.: Prentice-Hall, Inc., 1965. $7.95; text ed., $5.75.

The Sex Knowledge Inventories. Two forms: Form X, an objective measure of general sex knowledge; Form Y, an objective measure of anatomical and vocabulary knowledge. Available to professionally trained persons from Family Life Publications, Inc., Box 6725, College Station, Durham, N. C. 27700. Specimen set of Forms X and Y, $2.75.

Steward, Verne. *Are They Qualified for Marriage?* Minneapolis: T. S. Denison & Co., 1964. 168 pp. $3.50.

Organizations Offering Assistance

American Association for Health, Physical Education, and Recreation. National Education Association, 1201 16th St. N. W., Washington, D. C. 20036.

American Medical Association, Department of Community Health and Health Education, 535 N. Dearborn St., Chicago, Ill. 60610.

American Social Health Association, 1790 Broadway, New York, N. Y. 10019.

Child Study Association of America, 9 E. 89th St., New York, N. Y. 10028.

Commission on Family Life, National Council of the Churches of Christ in the U. S. A., 475 Riverside Dr., New York, N. Y. 10027.

National Council on Family Relations, 1219 University Ave. S. E., Minneapolis, Minn. 55414.

Sex Information and Education Council of Canada, 20 St. Joseph St., Suite 2, Toronto 5, Ontario.

Sex Information and Education Council of the U. S. (SIECUS), 1790 Broadway, New York, N. Y. 10019. *SIECUS Newsletter,* quarterly, $2 per year.

Addresses of Publishers and Producers

Abelar-Schuman, Ltd., 6 W. 57th St., New York, N. Y. 10019

Abingdon Press, 201 Eighth Ave. S., Nashville, Tenn. 37203

American Medical Association, Department of Community Health and Health Education, 535 N. Dearborn St., Chicago, Ill. 60610

Appleton-Century-Crofts, Inc., 440 Park Ave. S., New York, N. Y. 10016

Association Press, 291 Broadway, New York, N. Y. 10007

Augsburg Publishing House, 426 S. Fifth St., Minneapolis, Minn. 55415

Ballantine Books, Inc., 630 Fifth Ave., New York, N. Y. 10020

Barron's Educational Series, Inc., 343 Great Neck Rd., Great Neck, N. Y., 11020

Basic Books, Inc., 404 Park Ave. S., New York, N. Y. 10016

Belmont Books, Inc., 66 Leonard St., New York, N. Y. 10013

Concordia Publishing House, 3558 S. Jefferson Ave., St. Louis, Mo. 63118

Concordia Tract Mission, Box 201, St. Louis, Mo. 63166

T. S. Denison & Co., Inc., 321 Fifth Ave. S., Minneapolis, Minn. 55415

Doubleday & Co., Inc., 501 Franklin Ave., Garden City, L. I., N. Y. 11531

E. P. Dutton & Co., 201 Park Ave. S., New York, N. Y. 10003

Wm. B. Eerdmans Publishing Co., 255 Jefferson Ave. S. E., Grand Rapids, Mich. 49502

Fortress Press, 2900 Queen Lane, Philadelphia, Pa. 19129

Golden Press, Inc., 850 Third Ave., New York, N. Y. 10022

Hammond Publishing Co., 115 E. Wells St., Milwaukee, Wis. 53202

Harcourt, Brace and World, Inc., 757 Third Ave., New York, N. Y. 10017

Harper & Row, 49 E. 33d St., New York, N. Y. 10016

Herald Press, 610 Walnut Ave., Scottdale, Pa. 15683

Inor Publishing Co., 210 Lexington Ave., Sweet Springs, Mo. 65351

Inter-Varsity Press, 1519 N. Astor, Chicago, Ill. 60610

Lutheran Church Press, 2900 Queen Lane, Philadelphia, Pa. 19129

The Macmillan Co., Inc., 60 Fifth Ave., New York, N. Y. 10011

The McGraw-Hill Book Co., Inc., 330 W. 42d St., New York, N. Y. 10036

Medical Research Press, 136 W. 52d St., New York, N. Y. 10019

Julian Messner, Inc., 8 W. 40th St., New York, N. Y. 10018

Meredith Press, 1716 Locust St., Des Moines, Iowa 50303

Monona Publications, 803 Moygara Rd., P. O. Box 3222, Madison, Wis. 53704

Thomas Nelson & Sons, Copewood & Davis Sts., Camden, N. J. 08103

Prentice-Hall, Inc., Englewood Cliffs, N. J. 07631

Public Affairs Pamphlets, 381 Park Ave. S., New York, N. Y. 10016

Science Research Associates, Inc., 259 E. Erie St., Chicago, Ill. 60611

Charles Scribner's Sons, Vreeland Ave., Totowa, N. J. 07500

Seabury Press, Inc., 815 Second Ave., New York, N. Y. 10017

San Diego City Schools, San Diego, Calif. 92100

Simon and Schuster, Inc., 1 W. 39th St., New York, N. Y. 10018

State Publishing Co., 6715 W. Florissant Ave., St. Louis, Mo. 63136

Zondervan Publishing Co., 1415 Lake Dr. S. E., Grand Rapids, Mich. 49506